WK 784

Cirencester College Library
Fosse Way Campus
S
C
G

D1331318

Baroque Music

IN FOCUS

Hugh Benham

SECOND EDITION

R·

Cirencester College, GL7 1XA
Telephone: 01285 640994

CIRCENCE
WIT
347319

cirencester
college
a beacon college

Music Study Guides

GCSE, AS and A2 Music Study Guides (AQA, Edexcel and OCR)
GCSE, AS and A2 Music Listening Tests (AQA, Edexcel and OCR)
GCSE Music Study Guide (WJEC)
GCSE Music Listening Tests (WJEC)
AS/A2 Music Technology Study Guide (Edexcel)
AS/A2 Music Technology Listening Tests (Edexcel)
Revision Guides for GCSE (AQA, Edexcel and OCR), AS and A2 Music (Edexcel)

Also available from Rhinegold Education

Key Stage 3 Listening Tests: Book 1 and Book 2
AS and A2 Music Harmony Workbooks
GCSE and AS Music Composition Workbooks
GCSE and AS Music Literacy Workbooks
Romanticism in Focus, Baroque Music in Focus, Film Music in Focus, Modernism in Focus,
The Immaculate Collection in Focus, *Who's Next* in Focus, *Batman* in Focus,
Goldfinger in Focus, Musicals in Focus, Music Technology from Scratch

Rhinegold also publishes Choir & Organ, Classical Music, Classroom Music,
Early Music Today, International Piano, Music Teacher, Muso, Opera Now, Piano, The Singer,
Teaching Drama, British and International Music Yearbook, British Performing Arts Yearbook,
British Music Education Yearbook, World Conservatoires,
Rhinegold Dictionary of Music in Sound

Other Rhinegold Study Guides

Rhinegold publishes resources for candidates studying Drama and Theatre Studies.

First published 2010 in Great Britain by
Rhinegold Education
239–241 Shaftesbury Avenue
London WC2H 8TF

Telephone: 020 7333 1720
Fax: 020 7333 1765

www.rhinegold.co.uk

© Rhinegold Publishing Ltd 2010

All rights reserved. No part of this publication may be reproduced, stored in a retrieval
system, or transmitted in any form or by any means, electronic, mechanical, photocopying,
recording or otherwise, without the prior permission of Rhinegold Publishing Ltd.
This title is excluded from any licence issued by the Copyright Licensing Agency, or other
Reproduction Rights Organisation.

Rhinegold Publishing Ltd has used its best efforts in preparing this guide. It does not assume,
and hereby disclaims, any liability to any party for loss or damage caused by errors or
omissions in the guide whether such errors or omissions result from negligence, accident or
other cause.

Baroque Music in Focus (2nd edition)

British Library Cataloguing in Publication Data.
A catalogue record for this book is available from the British Library.

ISBN: 978-1-906178-88-8

Printed in Great Britain by Headley Brothers Ltd

CONTENTS

The author

Hugh Benham is a chair of examiners for GCE Music, organist, writer, and former teacher. He contributed to *The New Grove Dictionary of Music and Musicians* (2001) and is the author of two books on English church music, one of which (*John Taverner: his life and music*) was published by Ashgate in 2003. He has contributed to *Music Teacher* and *Classroom Music* magazines, has written articles on early music, and was the editor of Taverner's complete works for *Early English Church Music* (published by Stainer and Bell for The British Academy).

Acknowledgments

The author wishes to thank Lucien Jenkins for his support and assistance during the preparation of this book, and Alistair Wightman for his advice and suggestions.

Grateful thanks also to Sarah Smith, Elisabeth Boulton, Ben Robbins, Emma Findlow, Zoë Franklin, Chris Elcombe, Adrian Horsewood, Harriet Power, Ben Smith, Alex Stevens, Silvia Schreiber and Hal Bannister of Rhinegold Publishing for their assistance during the editing and production process.

I. INTRODUCTION

There is a vast amount of Baroque music to cram into one short book – in fact most Western classical music composed between about 1600 and 1750. The music is amazingly varied. Some was for dancing, some for entertainment, some for education and some was written to the glory of God. It continues to have a strong effect – it can be exciting, charming, relaxing. This book has been written to introduce you to it and to try to explain its unique qualities, and of course what makes it all, despite so much variety, 'Baroque'.

Listening

Music is composed to be performed and listened to. The point of reading books about it is to learn to hear things that we might otherwise miss. But reading about music is not easy – no writer can translate a musical experience into words. So a good plan is to listen, read, listen again (and then if necessary reread and re-listen).

Listening is the key, so do listen to a range of recordings as well as to Classic FM and BBC Radio 3, and attend live concerts. In particular, this book offers various suggestions for listening, based on three compilation CDs:

- ■ *World of Early Music* (Naxos 8.554770–71), 2 CDs: WEM
- ■ *Discover Music of the Baroque Era* (Naxos 8.558160–61), 2CDs: DMBE
- ■ *Favourite Baroque Classics* (Helios CDH55020): FBC.

> Tracks are identified by the initials of the compilation, number of CD (if more than one), track number. WEM 1: 19, for example, means *World of Early Music* CD 1, track 19. WEM 2: 2 means CD 2, track 2, and so on.

You don't have to opt for these particular recordings, as everything is available in other recordings; we've chosen these as you're likely to find them good value and easy to get hold of. Remember that recordings of some items not represented in the compilation CDs may be available on YouTube, iTunes, Spotify or from Naxos Music Library.

Years and centuries

We often need to mention particular years and centuries. The system of reference works like this: because years 1 to 99 were the 1st century, 2010 is part of the 21st century. So Bach (1685–1750) was born in the 17th century and died half way through the 18th.

Abbreviations and Roman numerals

We refer to Bach's works with the letters 'BWV' and a number. The letters 'BWV' stand for 'Bach-Werke-Verzeichnis' – German for 'Bach-works-index'. Bach's works are often identified by BWV numbers, especially when there are two or more with similar titles.

Some dates are marked 'c.', which stands for the Latin word 'circa', meaning 'about'; it means we don't know the exact date. You'll also find a few marked 'r.', which stands for 'reigned'. These are always to do with kings or queens, in cases where it is more useful to know when they were in power than when they were alive.

We occasionally use Roman numerals. For 1–10, these run I, II, III, IV, V, VI, VII, VIII, IX, X.

2. BACH'S AIR IN D

Listening must come first. So we begin with one of the most widely known of all pieces of music, Bach's Air in D from his Orchestral Suite No 3 (FBC: 2).

When you listen to this music, you will hear that it:

- Is fairly slow
- Is played by violins and other stringed instruments
- Has a violin melody with a mixture of long held notes and shorter ones
- Has a bass part that moves in equal notes, with alternating large leaps and small steps.

Listen again, and you should also notice that:

- The melody and bass *together* are the most important parts
- Another instrument plays with the strings – it plays an accompaniment, not a solo part

In FBC: 2 this is a theorbo, a type of lute.

- The mood is much the same throughout – there are no sharp contrasts.

Several of these features are typical of Baroque music, so you'll meet them again. That's one good reason for listening carefully: every time you notice features in a piece, you're better prepared to understand how the next piece you hear works.

The Air in D began life as the second movement (or piece) in a suite (or collection of pieces) which Bach wrote in about 1730. 'Air' is a French word for 'song' – like some other German composers, Bach was influenced by French music, especially dance music. He clearly felt that his piece, although not sung, had song-like qualities.

The piece was much admired in the 19th century, and the violinist August Wilhelmj made an arrangement for solo violin and piano. He transposed Bach's melody down by an octave and one note so that it could be played entirely on the lowest (G) string of the violin, to feature the rich sound typical of that string. That's how its nickname – 'Air on the G string' – came about. But with FBC: 2 and other modern recordings you'll hear the Air in its original version, with the brighter sound that Bach himself expected.

3. PUTTING THINGS IN CONTEXT

Western Europe

The music referred to in this book was composed in western Europe, almost entirely in Italy, Germany, France and England. There was plenty of Baroque music in other European countries, including Spain, Poland and Denmark, and in parts of the Spanish Empire in America (notably Mexico and Peru), but as this is a short book, we've had to leave the music of these countries aside.

The map of Europe looked different in the 17th and early 18th centuries from how it looks now. It also changed a great deal *during* this time, chiefly as a result of war: the map below shows how Europe looked after the Treaty of Westphalia in 1648, which ended several long-running wars that had involved all the major powers in Continental Europe.

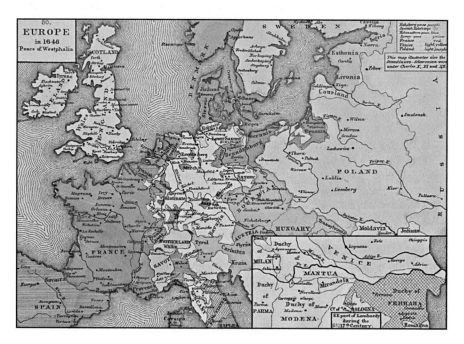

There was then no single country called Italy. In 1648, for example, the area now called Italy included the republic of Venice (about the size of southern England), the Papal States (a large area, including Rome, ruled by the Pope), Tuscany (with its capital at Florence), Genoa, and the large southern Spanish-controlled kingdom of Naples (with Sicily).

Modern Germany was part of the Holy Roman Empire, a federation of more or less self-governing states, some Catholic, some Protestant. The empire also included modern Belgium, Austria, the Czech Republic, parts of Poland and northern Italy.

Scotland and England began the Baroque period as two separate countries, but joined monarchies in 1603 and parliaments in 1707.

Government, wealth and religion

The states of western Europe did not have democratically elected governments. Although King Louis XIV of France (r. 1643–1715) probably didn't say *'L'Etat, c'est moi'* ('I am the state'), the tradition that this was his view does make clear that kings didn't expect to be challenged. Accordingly the best music in France was centred on the royal court at Versailles, near Paris.

Britain was a slightly different case, since the crown *was* challenged and the king beheaded halfway through the 17th century; after that British kings and queens became better at compromising!

Wealth was unevenly distributed. Most land and property belonged to kings, aristocrats and churches, but many other people were poor. Nevertheless, in some societies (including Great Britain), the middle classes were increasingly prosperous – and music was one thing that many of them liked to spend their money on.

Western Europe was almost entirely Christian. The church in some areas (such as Italy and France) was Roman Catholic, while in others (including parts of Germany) it was Protestant. The Church of England combined Catholic and Protestant elements. There was little religious choice or tolerance, and many wars were at least partly wars of religion, including the Thirty Years' War in Germany between Catholics and Protestants. But although the influence of religion was much greater and more far-reaching than nowadays, it was already in slow decline. Less music was written for the church in the Baroque period than previously, and more for secular (non-church) purposes.

In Catholic countries church services were in Latin; elsewhere they were generally in the local language. So as a rough and ready rule, most church music setting Latin words was written by composers in Catholic countries. But life is never that simple, and Latin was sometimes used in the Lutheran church in Germany, for example, which was Protestant. Two major works by Bach, his Magnificat in D and B minor Mass, both have Latin texts. The types of music composed depended on local circumstances – for example, works based on chorales (German hymn tunes) were for the German Lutheran church.

How (and what) Baroque music survived

Before recording and broadcasting were invented in the 19th and 20th centuries, music could be passed on from one person to another live (the notes by performance and the instructions by word of mouth), or on paper (in writing or in print). The Baroque music that survives today has come down to us on paper. Starting from materials in museums and libraries, modern publishers have made much of it available in easy-to-use editions: a great deal has been performed from these editions, and record companies have issued thousands of CDs (many of which we can hear in radio broadcasts). Baroque music is also widely available on YouTube, iTunes, Spotify and via the Naxos Music Library.

The music that *wasn't* written down is largely lost to us now, including most that was used and enjoyed by less privileged people. So the Baroque music we know today is almost entirely the music played and listened to by the upper and middle classes. A lot of written and printed music by outstanding composers like Monteverdi and Bach has also been lost, perhaps because people in the 17th and 18th centuries had an attitude to yesterday's music a bit like ours to yesterday's computer: interesting, but not as useful or as exciting as the latest model.

4. COMPOSERS, PERFORMERS AND LISTENERS

Although so much was different in Baroque times, then as now there was no music without composers, performers and listeners. Bear in mind that roles overlapped: many musicians were active as composers and performers – J. S. Bach was an organist, for instance, and Purcell a singer.

Composers

Composers did not think of themselves as great artists dedicated to expressing their innermost feelings through music as some later musicians have done. They were first and foremost working musicians with livings to make. Often, they were paid to compose music for wealthy and influential people and organisations – for royalty, the aristocracy, the authorities of prosperous cities, or the church. J. S. Bach worked for years for the church in Leipzig; his bosses did not think he was anyone special.

Such people and organisations were aware of the prestige that music could bring, and of how it could show off their wealth and status at public and private functions. This system is termed patronage, the patron being the person who employed the composer. Louis XIV of France was Lully's patron, for example, and from 1717 to 1723 Prince Leopold of Anhalt-Cöthen was J. S. Bach's.

Louis XIV of France, Lully's patron

Publishing was an important source of income for some composers. The most important commercial publisher, with an international trade, was the Frenchman Estienne Roger (1665/6–1722) of Amsterdam (Netherlands), whose firm published music by, among others, the Italian composers Corelli and Vivaldi. Publishers not only printed the music, but also sold it on behalf of the composer, who received payment for it. Much music was published in manuscript by professional music copyists. A lack of effective copyright meant that pirated editions of a composer's work were sometimes issued, for which the composer received nothing.

Composers were usually from middle-class backgrounds. The least well-off in society had few opportunities to train as musicians. The wealthiest didn't earn their living in a trade – nevertheless, the Holy Roman Emperor Leopold I (1640–1705), was among several royal and aristocratic people who composed excellent music, and some other wealthy patrons were amateur performers.

Jobs (including music jobs) were often handed down from father to son: Bach was born into a family whose business had been music for several generations; the Couperin family had a leading role in French music for many years.

Some composers, including Bach and Handel, were expert improvisers. Improvising is sometimes described as making up a piece as you go along – composing and performing at the same time. But, like jazz musicians, Bach and Handel knew from experience broadly how each piece would work – it was the detail that was not planned in advance. Improvised pieces were not written down, but were heard once and then generally forgotten. But some surviving music does sound as if it began life as an improvisation, for example, the beginning of Bach's famous organ Toccata in D minor (BWV 565) with its impetuous succession of different musical ideas and simple but dramatic textures.

Elisabeth-Claude Jacquet de la Guerre

Finally, were there women composers at this time? There certainly were some, including the Italians Francesca Caccini (1587–c. 1641) – daughter of the composer Giulio Caccini – and Barbara Strozzi (1619–1677), and Elisabeth-Claude Jacquet de la Guerre (1665–1729) in France. But composing was largely a male business. Several of J. S. Bach's sons became composers, but apparently none of his daughters did. Although society was becoming less inflexible, it was still restrictive. There were strict rules about what was men's and what was women's work, and educational opportunities for girls and women were limited. The Baroque period saw the first professional women writers and actors, and some women performers of music (we mention a few in the next section), but relatively few composers and painters.

Performers

As there were no recordings, we can't tell exactly how Baroque singers and players sounded. But we do know that performers often added ornamentation, especially when a passage was repeated.

Accordingly, the solo violinist adds ornamentation in the repeats of Bach's Air in D on FBC: 2.

Keyboard continuo players weren't given fully written-out parts, but had to improvise accompaniments from a bass part, often with figures to indicate the chords required.

> For the word 'continuo', see Glossary and Chapter 6, section 'Basso continuo'.

Performers were given few dynamic markings to indicate, for example, loud or soft, few tempo (speed) indications and few details of articulation such as staccato. Composers provided these instructions only when really necessary or when you couldn't be sure from the character and style of the music how it should be played or sung. Composers assumed that musicians could work out what was needed; besides, they often dealt directly with performers.

Performers as well as composers were supported or employed by royal and aristocratic patrons. For example, the court orchestras of Kings Louis XIV of France and Charles II of England provided employment for considerable numbers of players. The Duke of Chandos, who employed Handel as composer-in-residence, had 20 or more first-class musicians working for him, including a brother of the Italian composer Alessandro Scarlatti and one of Bach's cousins.

It was during the Baroque period that the cult of the star performer was born, particularly in opera. In the 1720s, some of Handel's operas featured the famous and highly paid soprano Francesca Cuzzoni (1696–1778) and her rival the mezzo-soprano Faustina Bordoni (1697–1781). Both women were extremely temperamental, and once came to blows on the stage. Tickets for one of Cuzzoni's concerts in England cost 60 guineas (equivalent in purchasing power to well over £8,000 in the early 21st century).

Francesca Cuzzoni and Faustina Bordoni

Before the development of opera around 1600, women had not normally sung in public (it was considered rather immodest), and even through the Baroque period they had no regular place in church choirs (other than in convent choirs, of course). Boys sang the treble parts as they still sometimes do in church and cathedral choirs in the United Kingdom.

Instrument technology was advancing and with it the technical demands made on players. Instrument designs and playing techniques were not standardised as in more recent times. Some Baroque violinists, for example, held the instrument on the collar-bone as modern players do, while others held it at chest level. Some music was deliberately showy. For example, a visitor to Venice in 1715 remarked on a violin improvisation by Vivaldi with unusually high notes, incredibly fast playing and much multiple stopping. Vivaldi must have played a violin with an unusually long fingerboard for the time, since many 18th-century instruments didn't allow you to play much higher than the C two octaves above middle C.

Some performances were directed by a person beating time, either with a rolled-up piece of music paper or by thumping on the floor with a stick; Lully and other French conductors did this.* However, as most Baroque music involved fairly small numbers of performers, it wasn't always necessary to have a separate conductor. Often a keyboard or lute player would direct, perhaps occasionally managing by eye contact or a nod to signal an entry or a change of tempo, rather as modern chamber music players do. In Italy especially, the leading violinist in an orchestra would stand to direct the performance, keeping the players together by movements of his instrument or bow. No one used a baton as modern conductors do until the early 19th century.

> *Apparently, Lully hit himself on the foot with his conducting cane in 1687, the wound never healed, and he died three months later.

Many people played or sang for their own pleasure or for family and friends at home or in clubs and societies. Music was widely seen as a desirable accomplishment, especially for young ladies. However, not everyone thought so. The English philosopher John Locke disapproved of young men spending time on music: 'a good hand, upon some instruments, is by many people mightily valued. But it wastes so much of a young man's time … and engages often in such odd company, that many think it much better spared; and I have, amongst men of parts and business, so seldom heard any one commended or esteemed for having an excellency in music, that amongst all those things, that ever came into the list of accomplishments, I think I may give it the last place.' (John Locke, *Some Thoughts Concerning Education* (1693), section 197.)

Listeners

Nowadays we can hear music almost all the time. In the Baroque period there was far less music – no recordings and no television of course, but also few public concerts. Moreover, most Baroque musical events were open only to the privileged few, and many were by invitation. When in the late 1600s John Banister played violin in Charles II's string band, the audience consisted of the king and his court. When, on the other hand,

Banister organised public concerts in London, everyone was welcome who could afford the admission charge of one shilling.* Banister's London concerts were probably the first public concerts anywhere, although the first commercial opera house had been opened in Venice as early as 1637. Incidentally, the musical life of London continued to be rich and varied right through the first half of the 18th century.

*There were 20 shillings in the pound; but Banister's shilling (5p) would have had the buying power of over £6 in the early 21st century. On the other hand, a smaller proportion of the population had that amount to spare than today.

Anyone could hear music in church, but only a few churches had an ambitious musical programme. If you had been in Venice in the early 1600s you might have heard music by Giovanni Gabrieli at one of the big state occasions in church attended by the doge (the doge was Venice's president or city mayor; his title comes from 'dux', a Latin word for a military leader from which our word 'duke' also comes). Henry Purcell was the organist of Westminster Abbey in the late 1600s, and plenty of his music was sung at services there. When Bach was organist, Sunday morning services at St Thomas's church, Leipzig normally included one of his cantatas before the sermon.

5. BAROQUE MUSIC: WHAT IS IT?

The period

The Baroque period of music history:

■ Began around the year 1600, about 400 years ago (in other words, it came after the Renaissance)
■ Ended around 1750, about 250 years ago (in other words, it came before the Classical period).

Over such a long period of time, music changed a great deal. Listen to a piece from about 1600 by Monteverdi (WEM 2: 2) or Gabrieli (WEM 2: 6 / DMBE 1: 6), then one from the first half of the 18th century by J. S. Bach (DMBE 2: 8) or Handel (FBC: 4). Monteverdi and Gabrieli sound different from Bach and Handel. Of course we must remember that Bach wouldn't have understood if you'd told him he was a late-Baroque composer, or even a Baroque one. All these 'periods' were the later inventions of writers about music, but period labels are quite useful in helping us understand more about how music developed.

At both the beginning and the end of the Baroque period some composers, performers and audiences explored new styles well ahead of others who stuck with existing ones. So we can't set precise dates – nothing changed dramatically between 31 December 1599 and 1 January 1600, for example, or in the final hours of 1750 – that's why we frequently write 'about' and 'c.'.

The roots of Baroque music go back to the late 16th century, for example to music by Andrea Gabrieli (c. 1533–1585) from Venice.* His music was composed earlier than, for instance, much of the music of William Byrd (c. 1540–1623), an English composer who, though later, definitely belongs to the world of the Renaissance.

> *Andrea was Giovanni Gabrieli's uncle and teacher; as Giovanni is the better known, references simply to 'Gabrieli' always mean him.

The reason for saying that the Baroque period ended in 1750 is largely because Bach died in that year, and while Handel lived until 1759, he composed little after 1750. Some music that sounds Baroque was written well after 1750, for example some works by William Boyce (1711–1779), including the *Twelve Overtures*, composed mainly in the 1760s. Equally, some composers were writing music before 1750 which pointed ahead to Classical styles – for example, J.S. Bach's son Carl Philipp Emanuel (1714–1788) published his *Prussian* and *Württemberg* sonatas for keyboard in the early 1740s.

The word 'Baroque'

In the 19th century the word 'Baroque' was employed chiefly for the often complicated and fancy styles of architecture and art popular in Europe from the late 16th century to the early 18th. Since then it has come to be widely applied to the music of the same time, but is sometimes used today of anything that is highly or extravagantly ornamented or over-complicated.

Originally the word Baroque was used only in a disapproving way. Coming from the Portuguese 'barroco', which meant an irregular-shaped pearl, it implied a deformed version of something beautiful. For example, many people thought that 17th-century architecture was less 'correct', less balanced than the previous Renaissance architecture from which it had developed. The new styles were too florid, too bizarre, a bit overdone – in a word, Baroque.

Some early 17th-century music might indeed strike you as slightly bizarre if you know the serene sounds of late Renaissance music. For example, compare some of Monteverdi's music such as 'Possente spirto e formidabil nume' from his opera *Orfeo* (WEM 2: 2) with Palestrina's (WEM 1: 19).

> Monteverdi's title translates as 'Powerful spirit, formidable god': Orpheus, by his singing, lulls to sleep Charon (the ferryman who takes him to the underworld in search of his wife Euridice). Monteverdi provided a simple vocal part, and an alternative elaboration of it (probably to show how a singer might ornament the basic version). WEM 2: 2 has both versions, the simple one first, the elaboration at 1'13".

The Ecstasy of St Teresa, by Gianlorenzo Bernini, one of the leading Italian Baroque sculptors

But why should most music by Baroque composers like Bach and Handel be considered bizarre, deformed, and so on: surely it is too regularly patterned and disciplined? Listen again to Bach's Air in D, or to Handel's 'The Arrival of the Queen of Sheba' (from *Solomon*) (FBC 4), for example.

Remember that in music the word 'Baroque' is first and foremost a convenient word for the period between about 1600 and 1750: in other words, just because Bach and Handel are Baroque (period) doesn't mean they are Baroque (weird).

6. BAROQUE MUSIC: WHAT'S SPECIAL ABOUT IT?

We said at the start of this book that Baroque music is 'amazingly varied', and we tasted some of that variety in Chapter 5 when we contrasted Monteverdi and Gabrieli with Bach and Handel. But if it is so varied, why lump it all together into one period rather than divide it up into different periods with different names? What has it all got in common from the point of view of sound and musical technique?

People have in fact compromised by suggesting three separate *stages* or *phases* for the Baroque period: see Chapter 7.

Well, it's surprisingly difficult to find anything common to *all* Baroque music that's not present also in *some* non-Baroque music. In fact a more useful question might well be 'What's *special* about Baroque music?'.

What's special, then?

Baroque music is special because, when compared to earlier music we notice the following:

- A new importance for the melody and bass parts
- A new kind of bass part known as basso continuo
- Greater expressiveness, sometimes with a strong dramatic element
- First use of keys based on major and minor scales
- First systematic use of different styles to suit different situations
- Growing popularity of instrumental music
- Different ways of writing for instruments and for voices
- Important new genres – in particular: suite, sonata, concerto (both concerto grosso and solo concerto), opera, oratorio, cantata.

We'll discuss the first three points now and turn to the others later.

Melody and bass

When listening to Bach's Air in D (Chapter 2) we noticed that the melody and bass parts together are the most important. This is true of many Baroque pieces, but also of so much later music that today it seems unremarkable. It was more of a novelty in the early 1600s. In most Renaissance music the main musical interest had been shared more equally between four or more parts, including the middle ones.

Basso continuo

The Italian term 'basso continuo' (literally 'continuous bass') is often abbreviated to 'continuo'. It refers to an instrumental bass line:

- That is continuous
- That is found mostly in Baroque pieces
- Above which a keyboard or lute player performed an improvised accompaniment with appropriate harmony.

So a single bass line provided by the composer was turned into an accompaniment with complete harmony. (Something similar happens nowadays when a bass guitarist plays a bass line and a rhythm guitarist plays chords.) The continuo idea dates back to the monody style developed in about 1600 (see Chapter 8). Here the composer wrote out only his melody plus a bass part, but the audience heard complete harmony.

Strictly, a continuo accompaniment wasn't needed in some later Baroque music. For example, if the four string parts of Bach's Air in D are heard on their own, the harmony is complete anyway. In orchestral works, Bach, and other composers of that time, kept the keyboard or lute accompaniments partly because the player could direct the other performers. A continuo accompaniment was still harmonically *essential* in some music, however, as in arias where the composer notated just a vocal part and bass.

We have spoken of 'keyboard or lute' accompaniment. The continuo accompaniment had to involve someone who could play chords. This could be a keyboard player – often an organist in a piece for church use, a harpsichordist in a secular (non-church) piece – but a lute, archlute, or theorbo player might take part instead (see Chapter 12 for more on these three instruments).

Soprano Joanne Lunn accompanied on the lute by Elizabeth Pallett

Accompanists didn't have a fully notated accompaniment with all the notes they needed; they had to improvise. Sometimes they had just the bass part and were expected to know what were the best chords to use. Sometimes the composer provided figures to help them (but without telling them exactly how to arrange the various notes of each chord). These figures showed where they needed to play something other than an ordinary 5/3 or root position chord. For example, the figuring '6' represented a first inversion. This is because the most important thing about a first inversion is the 6th above the bass (although there is also a 3rd – hence the alternative name for a first inversion, which is 6/3, e.g. E–G–C with E as bass). The continuo part could be played by the keyboard or lute player on their own, but the bass line was usually doubled by one or more string players (for example viol, cello or bass violin), and sometimes bassoon(s) as well.

The following example shows part of a Baroque figured bass on a bass stave. This is the accompanist's left-hand part. The notes on the treble stave show the kind of right-hand part that might be added to fit the given figuring; they are printed small, in accordance with a common convention, so that people can see immediately that they are not the composer's own.

Corelli, Sonata in F major, Op. 5 No. 10, first movement (Preludio)

Expressiveness

In everyday life people often express emotions by how they look and behave – happiness by smiling, distress by crying. Music has its own methods of expressing emotions – tempo, dynamics, key, type of harmony (including extent of dissonance) – in ways that people understand, recognise and are affected by. For example, it can express violent anger by becoming faster, louder and harsher – it might go on to express renewed calm by becoming slower, softer and sweeter.

Baroque composers were much more concerned than earlier musicians with expressing emotions through music. Especially in the middle and late Baroque periods they often considered it most effective to establish a particular 'affection' (their word for mood or emotion) at the beginning of a piece and keep to it throughout. In vocal music it was suggested by the words being set, but instrumental music (including Bach's Air in D) expressed affections too. For us, this keeping to a single affection can seem dull after the exciting changes of emotion in later music. Baroque composers simply had a different attitude.

Keeping to a single affection meant that big contrasts of musical style within a piece were generally avoided. Many of Bach's pieces, for example, are fairly similar in rhythm throughout. The bass part of his Air in D is almost all in quavers, and although the melody is more varied there are no sudden or disorientating contrasts.

Listen now to Purcell's song 'When I am laid in earth' from his opera *Dido and Aeneas* (WEM 2: 12 / DMBE 1: 19). The heroine Dido, abandoned by her lover, is desperate and about to commit suicide. Purcell expresses her intense grief by writing slow music in a minor key throughout. He deliberately includes dissonance on the word 'trouble'. This is 'word-painting' – Purcell has matched a *detail* of the text and a piece of musical *detail* (in addition to responding more generally to his heroine's emotional turmoil).

Julia Gooding and Michael George as Dido and Aeneas (Act 3, before their final parting)

Much word-painting is cliché – like the falling scale on 'fall' in Aeneas' recitative 'If not for mine' from *Dido*. Notice also how anguished and broken Purcell's solo part is, with several jagged dotted rhythms and long rests (as if Dido can scarcely keep going), and emotional little melismas on 'ah!'.

Baroque music: what's special about it?

A melisma is a group of notes on a single syllable. Melismas were often used to emphasise dramatic or emotive words (as, for example, at 'darkness' in the recitative before 'When I am laid in earth').

Underlying everything is the ground bass (a melodic phrase repeated over and over in the lowest part). Ground basses were much used in the 17th century as a way of prolonging a mood. Purcell exploits his grief-stricken phrase (see the example below) to the full, endlessly emphasising Dido's tragedy. The musical code for grief is clear – downward movement in semitone steps. The phrasing of the solo part is often out of step with the phrasing of the ground bass. Almost certainly Purcell meant all this to add to our sense of unease.

Purcell, 'When I am laid in earth' from *Dido and Aeneas*, Act 3

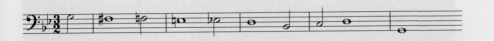

Quite different from Purcell's song is Handel's 'La Réjouissance' (French: 'Rejoicing') from *Music for the Royal Fireworks*. Handel represents rejoicing with a brisk tempo and simple, rather repetitive rhythms. The piece is in a major key throughout, with hardly a minor chord at all, and you won't find any chromatic writing. The melody is straight-forward and 'happy sounding'. You don't hear large or awkward intervals, but plenty of repetition (including many repeated-note patterns) and some sequences. (In a sequence a musical idea is repeated immediately at a different pitch.)

Listen now to some other mid- and late-Baroque pieces, and decide how the composer matches the ruling affection. One good place to start is Vivaldi's motet *In furore iustissimae irae* (Latin: 'In the fury of your most righteous anger'), which is about God's anger. How does Vivaldi depict the 'fury' and the 'anger'?

7. DIVIDING THE BAROQUE PERIOD

Early, middle and late

Because the Baroque period was so long and its music so varied, it is sometimes divided into three. The dates involved for these three stages are as approximate as those for the period as a whole.

The table below is for reference as you read on – look back to it whenever you need to.

Early Baroque (up to c. 1640/1650)	Middle Baroque (from c. 1640/1650 to c. 1690/1700)	Late Baroque (from c. 1690/1700 to c. 1750)
Composers include:	Composers include:	Composers include:
Giovanni Gabrieli (c. 1555–1612)	Jean-Baptiste Lully (1632–1687)	Antonio Vivaldi (1678–1741)
Claudio Monteverdi (1567–1643)	Arcangelo Corelli (1653–1713)	Johann Sebastian Bach (1685–1750)
Heinrich Schütz (1585–1672)	Henry Purcell (1659–1695)	George Frideric Handel (1685–1759)

If you listen to one piece by each composer you should get some idea of the differences between early, middle and late styles in Baroque music.

Of the three, late-Baroque music is the most widely known nowadays. Some of it, particularly music by Bach and Handel, has featured frequently in broadcasts and concerts for many years, and has been recorded many times. This started with a major revival of interest in late-Baroque music – especially Bach's – in the 19th century. It's no accident that the majority of 'favourite' pieces on FBC are from the late Baroque.

But much 17th-century music is full of excitement, passion and drama. Have you heard, for example, the ravishing love duet 'Pur ti miro, pur ti godo' (Italian: 'I adore you, I desire you') from *L'incoronazione di Poppea* ('The Coronation of Poppea')? (The opera is by Monteverdi, but this closing duet is probably by someone else, perhaps Francesco Sacrati, 1605–1650). Or try Purcell's anthem *Hear My Prayer* with its anguished ending (DMBE 1: 18).

Italian, French and German

As well as historical differences (changes over time), there were geographical differences (changes from place to place). We can identify different national styles in Baroque music, in particular Italian, French and German. See Chapters 9 and 13–18 for more on the nature of these national styles.

Dividing the Baroque period

For examples of middle- and late-Baroque Italian styles, listen to music by Corelli or Vivaldi (FBC: 14, 16). François Couperin (1668–1733) and Jean-Philippe Rameau (1683–1764) are among late-Baroque French composers (DMBE 2: 12 and FBC: 17). Organ music by Johann Pachelbel (1653–1706) and Dieterich Buxtehude (c. 1637–1707) is German in style. Listen to WEM 2: 19, 20, for a piece by each of these composers.

But bear in mind, as we noticed when we listened to Bach's Air in D, that national styles weren't always limited to their countries of origin. Handel is another example: he wrote opera in the Italian style (DMBE 2: 17) and overtures in the French style, as in *Messiah*, despite being born in Germany, and living and working in England for many years.

8. THE BEGINNINGS OF BAROQUE MUSIC

The Baroque period didn't start with a bang on 1 January 1600. But events in the Italian city of Florence just before that did lead to one of the biggest upheavals ever in music, and resulted in some of the first music that everyone agrees is Baroque and not Renaissance.

Florence

In the late 16th century most educated people in Italy had enormous respect for the ancient Greek civilisation and culture which had flourished 2,000 years previously. So it's not surprising that there was much interest in ancient Greek music among those Florentine musicians, poets and philosophers who met to sing and play music and discuss artistic matters. Some of these people belonged to a group known as the 'Camerata' – the word means 'society' or 'academy'.

Unfortunately, little if any ancient Greek music had survived. Nevertheless, Florentine musicians concluded that ancient Greek dramas were sung throughout, and that the words had governed the music. By contrast, the music of their own time* seemed to them over-complex, to the extent that it overshadowed the words.

*Listen, for example, to music by Giovanni Pierluigi da Palestrina (c. 1525–1594), Orlande de Lassus (c. 1532–1594) or Tomás Luis de Victoria (1548–1611), WEM 1: 19–21.

At the heart of most Renaissance music had been the complex interweaving of parts which we call counterpoint. Although the different voices fitted together well and produced pleasant harmony, each had a life of its own. It had its own melody, but above all its own rhythm – so that as you listened to the music you were aware of several parts moving independently, not just of a single block of sound. But although counterpoint may have been 'at the heart of most Renaissance music', not every passage was contrapuntal (the adjective formed from 'counterpoint'). In WEM 1: 19, can you hear the parts moving together in the section beginning at 0'40"?

In the 1580s, some musicians in Florence rejected counterpoint and attempted to write music which *would* put the words first in what they thought of as the ancient Greek manner. These attempts, principally by Vincenzo Galilei (the father of the scientist Galileo Galilei), do not survive.

The first operas

By 1600 musicians in Florence were composing extended dramas with singing throughout. They were not yet referred to as operas, but that's the obvious term for us to use. Two operas called *Euridice* were performed in 1600 and 1602. The first was mostly by Jacopo Peri (1561–1633) but partly by Giulio Caccini (1551–1618). The second is entirely by Caccini. Euridice was the wife of Orpheus, the great poet and musician of ancient Greek myth, so you can see the appeal of the story to composers.

In order that the words could be audible, Peri and Caccini stripped the texture down to one voice plus a simple continuo accompaniment of bass and chords almost throughout their operas. However, counterpoint survived and developed as the Baroque period went on, despite the writers of monody (for more, see Chapter 9, section 'Counterpoint').

Peri, Prologue from *Euridice*

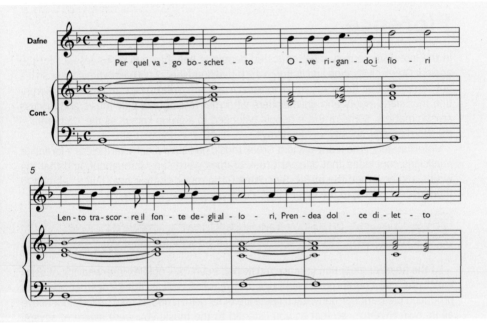

Peri was a good composer but not a great one, and his opera, although interesting, is quite hard going for modern audiences. Monteverdi, on the other hand, was one of the most outstanding musicians of all time. If you want a taste of early opera, listen to some of his *Orfeo* (1607). (See Chapter 16 for more on *Orfeo*.)

Monody

Nowadays the new single-voice-plus-continuo style is usually called 'monody'. People in the early 1600s often used the term *stile rappresentativo* (Italian: representational, or dramatic style).

Monody was sometimes heard outside opera. In 1601–1602 Caccini published a collection of songs entitled *Le nuove musiche* (Italian: 'new music'; the title tells us that Caccini was in no doubt that what he was doing was revolutionary). The music example below is a short excerpt from 'Amarilli, mia bella' (Italian: 'Amaryllis, my beautiful one'). Note, however, that singers would probably have ornamented what looks like a simple melody. The B♭ and F♯ in bar 2 make the melodic interval of a descending diminished 4th, a novel sound (this is *nuove musiche*, remember) in Caccini's time and much appreciated for its intensity by Baroque composers.

Caccini, 'Amarilli, mia bella' from *Le nuove musiche*

Some monody, like 'Amarilli, mia bella', is songlike, even tuneful, but other examples (including the one we gave under 'The first operas') are musically more basic – a kind of halfway-house between singing and speaking. This second kind of monody developed into the recitative style of later operas while more songlike monody is a forerunner of the later operatic aria. (You might like to think of rap, a singing style in which words also dominate the music to the extent that melody and accompaniment have virtually withered away.)

Monteverdi's 'Lament' from *Arianna* (1608), an opera otherwise lost, shows how expressive monody can be (WEM 2: 3 has an excerpt). In particular some dissonances are unprepared, as shown in the following music example. These were disapproved of by some early 17th-century critics, because they broke the traditional rules of counterpoint. Normally you did not move to a dissonance by a leap – you either moved by step from the note above or below, or you made the note that clashed a repeat of the non-dissonant note before it. Monteverdi clearly believed that such unprepared dissonances were justified if you were writing a lament portraying a heroine's heartfelt grief.

Monteverdi, 'Lasciatemi morire' (Italian: 'Let me die'), Lament from *Arianna**

*There is no figuring in this example. The keyboard realisation (i.e. completion) supplied here uses the chords implied by the bass and vocal parts.

Venice: contrasts

We began by emphasising the musical importance of Florence, but many important developments took place in Venice. In Renaissance times composers had sometimes scored some sections of long pieces for all the singers, others for smaller groups. And sometimes singers were divided into separate groups, on each side of the church, an antiphonal arrangement often referred to in Italian music as *cori spezzati* (Italian: 'separated choirs').

What was new and special in Venice in the last years of the 16th century was the use of more vivid contrasts, sometimes involving instruments and voices. Both Andrea and Giovanni Gabrieli played a major part in this. They worked at St Mark's, whose architecture, with several high galleries, made it possible to separate different groups of voices and instruments effectively and produce interesting 'stereo' effects.

Note that even when instruments and not singers are involved, we still use the term *cori spezzati*, because any group of performers, vocal or instrumental, was known as a 'coro' or 'choir'. Music with two or more contrasting 'choirs' is often referred to as polychoral.

For example, Giovanni Gabrieli's Christmas piece *Salvator noster* (Latin: 'Our Saviour') has three five-part choirs and continuo. One begins, before the other two together replace it. A dialogue between choirs I and III follows. After a repeat of the opening, we hear the magnificent sound of all three choirs together. Gabrieli uses these full forces sparingly – their sound would lose its impact if continued for too long.

In ecclesiis (Latin: 'In churches', meaning 'in every place where God's people gather') is an even more magnificent piece by the same composer for four solo singers, four-part choir, six-part instrumental choir of three cornetts,* viola and two trombones, and continuo. There are several sections for one or two solo singers and continuo, a short passage for instruments alone, and a triumphant ending for everyone.

*A cornett (double 't') was a wind instrument made of wood with a cup mouthpiece. It is not the ancestor of, and is quite different from, the modern brass cornet (single 't').

Interior of St Mark's, Venice, showing musicians' gallery

In the early 1600s a piece that combined voice(s) and instrument(s) was sometimes called a concerto, from an Italian word which can mean 'working together' – the meaning of a piece for soloist(s) and orchestra came later. Monteverdi's 'Nigra sum' (Latin: 'I am black'; the title and text are from the Bible, Song of Songs, chapter 1) is a concerto for tenor and basso continuo from his *Vespers* of 1610 . (For more on Monteverdi's *Vespers*, see page 86.)

Gabrieli's *In ecclesiis* and *Salvator noster* could be called 'concertos' too, but these were published in 1615 in a volume with the Latin title *Symphoniae sacrae* (Latin: 'Sacred symphonies'). The word 'symphonia' means literally a 'sounding together' of different groups of performers. The *Italian* word 'sinfonia' was sometimes used for an instrumental section within a work for voices and instruments.

Today we often speak of the *concertato* style when describing pieces which, like *In ecclesiis*, involve contrasts between different groups of performers. Some movements from Monteverdi's *Vespers*, including 'Dixit Dominus' (Latin: 'The Lord said'), are among other important examples of music in concertato style. The concertato style didn't necessarily involve large forces, but a basso continuo was always present.

Old and new: greater variety

17th-century Italian musicians didn't forget for a moment how different the new music was from the old. This shows up in some of the musical jargon of the time:

prima pratica = 'first practice' – referred to the 'old' Renaissance style which we associate with composers like Palestrina	**seconda pratica = 'second practice'** – monody, and some other music in which the 'rules' of the prima pratica have been disregarded in favour of a more striking treatment of the words (including some of Monteverdi's madrigals)
stile antico = 'antique style' – church music written in the 17th century which is still basically in the old-fashioned Renaissance style, with unaccompanied voices	**stile moderno = 'modern style'** – often refers to church music which is not antico, but more up-to-date, for voices and basso continuo (with or without other instruments)

The two practices could exist side by side, whereas previously there had been only one practice. More and more, music was made to fit the occasion for which it was intended. The late 17th-century writer Angelo Berardi (c. 1636–1694) noted in *Miscellanea Musica* (1689) that three types of music were now available, for the:

- Church
- Theatre
- Chamber.

He appears to imply that by contrast all Renaissance music was basically the same whatever its purpose. This is a bit of an exaggeration, but he was right to emphasise the new stylistic variety.

9. WHAT HAPPENED NEXT?

In a nutshell, this is what happened:

- Baroque styles spread widely
- Composers continued to use the 'melody and basso continuo' approach
- Despite this, counterpoint survived and developed
- A new approach to key and harmony was apparent by about 1670 (see Chapters 10–11)
- Many genres much used in later periods of classical music were developed.

Let's start with that first point. Baroque styles spread throughout Italy and to other areas of Europe. Major developments took place in Germany and France; England produced the outstanding composer Henry Purcell.

Italy

Opera was important throughout the Baroque period (Chapter 16). But we owe to the Italians other major genres, including the sonata and instrumental concerto (Chapters 14 and 15).

Although Italian composers were still numerous and influential in the early 18th century, it was from this time that Germans began to take the lead.

Germany

German composers from the first half of the 17th century included three Ss, handily born in consecutive years: Heinrich Schütz (1585–1672), Johann Hermann Schein (1586–1630) and Samuel Scheidt (1587–1654).

Schütz was a very important composer, the first from Germany to be widely known outside his own country. His *Psalmen Davids* (German: 'The Psalms of David', 1619) is a collection that built on the concertato style of his teacher Giovanni Gabrieli. 'Jauchzet dem Herren, alle Welt' (German: 'Shout for joy to the Lord, all the earth') is a suitably joyful setting of Psalm 100 for two four-part choirs and continuo (DMBE 1: 10). Schütz used monody in his *Kleine geistliche Concerte* (German: 'Little sacred concertos') of 1636–9; the downsizing implicit in that name resulted partly from economic problems caused by the Thirty Years' War – the assembling of large groups of performers had become difficult. Schütz lived to a great age, well into the middle Baroque, but his music is principally early Baroque in character. One of his most striking and attractive compositions is the *Historia der Geburt Jesu Christi* (a mixture of German and Latin: 'The story of the birth of Jesus Christ', a work widely known as the 'Christmas Story'). There is more on this in Chapter 17.

Schein and Scheidt both included German hymn melodies (chorales) in works based on the new Italian styles. Chorales continued to be important in German music, notably in J. S. Bach's church cantatas. Many organ pieces, usually known as organ chorales or chorale preludes, were based on them, by Bach and numerous other composers, including Pachelbel and Buxtehude (who worked mainly in Germany, but was of Danish birth). In Buxtehude's organ chorale 'Nun komm der Heiden Heiland' (German: 'Now come, Saviour of the heathen', WEM 2: 20) the melody is heard in the right hand – in a highly ornamented form – while the left hand and pedals accompany. In some organ chorales the melody can be heard much more clearly – without elaboration, as for example in Bach's 'Wachet auf, ruft uns die Stimme' (German: 'Wake up, the voice calls us').

St Mary's church in Lübeck, where Buxtehude was organist for nearly 40 years

By the early 18th century, the two composers now usually regarded as the most outstanding were of German birth – J. S. Bach and Handel. However, Georg Philipp Telemann, who produced an enormous amount of music in his long life (1681–1767), was regarded in his day as the leading German composer and is still much performed.*

*Listen for example to FBC: 21, 22 and DMBE 2: 11.

France

In the 17th century French music was centred chiefly on the royal court. The man who established a genuinely French Baroque style, and French opera independent of the Italian tradition, was actually an Italian: born Giovanni Battista Lulli in 1632, he died Jean-Baptiste Lully in 1687.

The music of Marc-Antoine Charpentier (c. 1645/50–1704) includes some important church works (WEM 2: 14). The orchestral prelude to one of these, the *Te Deum* in D, is a bright ceremonial piece in the form of a rondeau. 'Te Deum' is Latin for 'We praise you, God'; it is a song of thanksgiving and praise used on special occasions, such as a coronation or a victory. The Prelude has been used in recent years as the Eurovision signature tune (FBC: 1).

Jean-Philippe Rameau (1683–1764) composed operas and other works for the stage. In the French tradition, these contained plenty of dance pieces, for which Rameau is now best known (FBC: 17, 18 and DMBE 2: 14).

The leading French composer of keyboard music was François Couperin (1668-1733). His pieces are mainly based on dances, and usually are called after people he knew (DMBE 2: 13) or carry descriptive titles (DMBE 2: 12) rather than having abstract titles such as 'sonata' or 'prelude and fugue' in the German and Italian manner. Their 'prettiness' points ahead to the delicate rococo styles of the mid-18th century. 'Rococo' was a style emphasising elegance, lightness, even frivolity in the visual arts and music; it is first found in early 18th-century France.

England

In the early 17th century some English composers such as William Byrd and Orlando Gibbons (1583–1625) continued with styles developed in the time of Queen Elizabeth I (r. 1558–1603). But early 17th-century Italian developments had their effect on the younger generation, including the fine composer William Lawes (1602–1645, DMBE 1: 11), and Walter Porter (c. 1590–1659), a minor figure who is thought to have studied with Monteverdi.

The Civil War of the 1640s and the Commonwealth (1649–1660) were difficult times for music. The first English opera, *The Siege of Rhodes*, does however date from 1656. The music, contributed by five different composers, including William Lawes' brother Henry (1596–1662), no longer survives. Music became popular again at the court of Charles II (r. 1660–1685), particularly through the work of John Blow (1649–1708) and his pupil Henry Purcell (1659–1695), by far the most outstanding English Baroque composer.

Purcell was not just a court composer. He wrote much music for the theatre (public theatres, which were closed under the Commonwealth, reopened in the reign of Charles II). His semi-operas (dramatic works with some spoken sections), included *The Fairy Queen* (FBC: 10) and *The Indian Queen*. Thomas Betterton, the actor-manager, helped to establish this genre, which was influenced by contemporary French opera, and by the perceived English dislike of the continuous singing typical of Italian opera.

Purcell's only real opera, *Dido and Aeneas* (see pages 21–22), was probably first performed in a girls' school. Much of Purcell's music shows Italian and French influence (DMBE 1:19 / WEM 2: 12 and FBC: 10,11 respectively), but some other pieces, notably the Fantasias for viols (WEM 2: 16) which have no basso continuo part, were built on older, pre-Baroque English traditions.

A contemporary etching by William Hogarth of a scene from John Gay's *The Beggar's Opera*

Handel was a dominant figure in English music after he moved from Germany in the 1710s. His Italian operas were popular for a time, and later he established the English oratorio tradition (for opera and oratorio, see Chapters 16 and 17). England, and especially London, then one of the largest cities in the world and a prosperous one, attracted many foreign musicians. English-born musicians were also active, but among them there was no composer of really major importance, though it's worth noting John Gay (1685–1732), who composed *The Beggar's Opera* (1728), a ballad opera which enjoyed considerable success. Ballad operas were essentially plays in English with short songs, often using tunes popular at the time. The subject matter was sometimes racy and satirical, and some considered that ballad operas were liable to corrupt the young. They have more in common with modern musicals than with opera, and perhaps even some similarity to satirical television and radio programmes that use gags and songs to mock politicians and celebrities.

Counterpoint

As we saw in Chapter 8, some early Baroque composers rejected counterpoint in favour of monody. It didn't disappear altogether of course, as the beginning of Gabrieli's *Salvator noster* demonstrates. In fact it is very important in some Baroque music – especially in Germany, and above all in the works of J. S. Bach.

The problems of counterpoint versus clear word-setting which the first Baroque composers identified didn't of course apply to instrumental music, and in vocal pieces composers learned how to project words clearly even in contrapuntal passages, notably through frequent repetition. Listen, for example, to the closing chorus of Purcell's *Dido and Aeneas*, or to choruses from Handel's *Messiah*. The words are generally clearly audible – and each composer's attention to the *affection* of the words gives us powerful clues to meaning in any case.

Baroque counterpoint did not just follow Renaissance models. As a broad generalisation:

- In Renaissance music the *counterpoint produced the harmony* – the various interweaving melodic lines formed chords as they went along
- In Baroque music *harmony governed the counterpoint* – the composer thought harmonically and fitted the counterpoint to it.

As an example of Bach's counterpoint, listen to one of his keyboard fugues, perhaps one of the 48 from *Das wohltemperierte Klavier* ('The Well-tempered Clavier') such as the G minor from Book 1 (DMBE 2: 7, beginning at 1'51"). 'The Well-tempered Clavier' consists of two sets of 24 preludes and fugues. Each set has preludes and fugues in all 24 available keys, major and minor. The keys with most sharps and flats had generally been avoided by composers as some intervals and chords sounded out of tune. New systems of tempering (tuning) keyboard instruments now made these keys usable.

A fugue is a contrapuntal piece based on a short melody heard at the start. This melody is taken up in turn – or imitated – by the various parts (or 'voices', as parts in a fugue are often called even when not sung). It returns from time to time, in different keys. Fugues can be quick or slow, long or short, cheerful or serious – the basic fugal method just described can be elaborated in countless ways.

A canon, a type of contrapuntal composition, is similar to a round such as *Frère Jacques* or *London's Burning*. Two or more voices (or groups of voices) sing the same tune all the way through, but starting at different times. In other words, the second and later groups imitate the first exactly throughout. Bach was the most expert writer of canons (there are fine examples in his *Goldberg* variations, for example). But Pachelbel's Canon in D (FBC: 3) for three violins and continuo is the best known Baroque canon – in fact it's probably the best known of all Baroque pieces (and one which has been much arranged, adapted and borrowed from in recent years, for example in 1995 by Oasis in *Don't Look Back in Anger*).

When you listen to the start of Pachelbel's piece, can you hear the three violin parts entering in turn to make the canon, over an independent bass part? Remember, however, that some published arrangements of Pachelbel's Canon are much simplified: it may be impossible to tell from these versions that the piece is a canon at all.

Early, middle and late

To summarise:

Period	Dates	Developments	Examples
Early Baroque	c. 1600 to c. 1640/1650	Discovery and experiment	Birth of basso continuo, monody and concertato style
Middle Baroque	c. 1640/1650 to c. 1690/1700	Development and growth	Development of the major-minor key system
Late Baroque	c. 1690/1700 to c. 1750	Ripeness and maturity	Work of J. S. Bach and Handel

10. MAJOR AND MINOR KEYS

Keys and scales

One of the most important things that happened in the Baroque period was the development of a system of keys based on major and minor scales. Most pieces composed between about 1670 and the end of the 19th century used this system, and many still do.

From modes to scales

Major and minor scales evolved from older types of scales called modes. This complicated process, which began during the Renaissance, was basically as follows:

■ Modes with a major 3rd above note 1 developed into major scales. These modes are often referred to nowadays as the Lydian, Mixolydian, and Ionian modes.
■ Modes with a minor 3rd above note 1 developed into minor scales. These modes were the Dorian, Phrygian and Aeolian.

> The Glossary has a little more on the modes referred to here (see 'Modes').

This process of evolution from modes to major and minor scales was subtly linked with the invention of the basso continuo and the new two-part melody-and-bass textures. Composers were now more concerned with controlling the sounds between parts (partly for expressive purposes). In other words, they thought more and more in terms of chords – they were less happy just to let the harmony come about, as a kind of by-product, from the movement of various melodic lines. As time went on, this tighter, more systematic control led composers to prefer the relatively narrow harmonic range resulting from use of major and minor scales, keys and functional harmony, to the wider but less focused possibilities of the old modes.

In early Baroque music one sign of still fairly unsystematic harmony is the use of contradictory notes (such as F♮ and F♯) in succession in different parts ('false relations'). In the following music example, from Monteverdi's madrigal *Ohimè, se tanto amate* ('Alas, if you love so much'), look out for the B♭–B♮, F♮–F♯ and E♭–E♮ false relations.

Monteverdi, *Ohimè, se tanto amate*

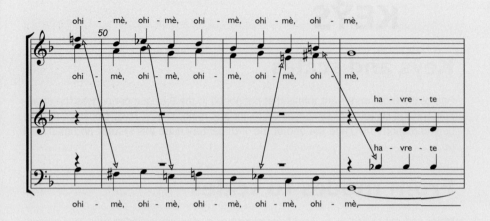

Harmony in major and minor keys

In a major or minor key, the tonic (note 1 of the scale) is used widely, and normally occurs at the end to give a feeling of completeness, of arriving home. It sounds 'central' or 'home-like' partly because of the system of harmony usually employed in music that is in a major or minor key. Each chord has a special function in establishing and supporting the key – especially the chords whose roots (lowest notes) are notes 1, 5 and 4 of the scale (these are usually known by Roman numerals as chords I, V and IV). The whole system is often termed 'functional harmony'.

Chord I is the tonic or home chord, just as note 1 of the scale is the tonic or home note. Chords I and V (the dominant) together are able in a unique way to get us into, and keep us in, a key, especially when in the order V–I, which forms a perfect cadence. Chord IV (the subdominant) provides contrast to I and V, sometimes, for example, acting as a kind of preparation for chord V in a perfect cadence.

Chromatic and diatonic

It's possible to use occasional notes from outside a major or minor scale and still be in the key belonging to that scale. One C♯ may not take us out of G major, for example. Occasional out-of-key notes are chromatic (the ordinary scale notes are diatonic).

Modulation

However, the repeated use of C♯ (provided that the other notes of the G major scale stay the same) takes us out of G major into D major, whose scale is D–E–F♯–G–A–B–C♯–D. The process of changing key is modulation. Some modulations are more important than others. In particular you can stay in a new key for quite a long time, or just pass through it.

In the Baroque period composers usually modulated to keys closely related to the tonic key. In other words, they tended to go only to keys whose scales had a similar number of sharps and flats. If they began in D major (two sharps), they would visit A major (three sharps) or B minor (two sharps) rather than, for example, Db major (five flats). The key whose signature has one sharp more (or one flat fewer) than the tonic is the 'dominant key'. To put it another way, A major is the dominant key of D major, because A is the dominant note (note 5) of D major. Among other keys closely related to D major are the subdominant, G major, and the relative minor, B minor.

Composers tended to use a relatively small range of keys partly because most systems of tuning keyboard instruments led to some keys sounding out of tune (see the comment on tuning above, under 'Counterpoint' in Chapter 9). Occasionally problems could be alleviated by use of 'split keys' (see picture below): for example, some early keyboard instruments had one part of a black key for D♯, the other for E♭, rather than having a single key for both sounds as we do today.

Italian virginal, c. 1620, with split keys

11. KEYS AND FORM

Baroque composers used carefully planned changes of key to give clear form (i.e. shape or structure) to their music.

Binary form

Many Baroque pieces, especially those based on dances, are in binary form, so called because there are *two* clearly separated sections, each usually repeated (think of binary in maths, with the *two* numbers, 0 and 1). The letters A B (or A A B B) are sometimes used to describe binary form in music. The two sections may be similar in length, or the second may be longer.

This is how the key structure usually works in binary form:

Section A	begins in the	tonic key
Section A	usually ends in	another key – the dominant (or perhaps if the starting key is minor, the relative major)
Section B	usually goes through	key(s) not previously heard
Section B	ends in the	tonic key

Pachelbel's Gigue in D (FBC: 3, beginning at 3'24") is in binary form. It's easy to hear where the sections and their repeats end, because this is the only time that the music pauses for breath. Section A begins in D major and ends in the dominant key, A major. Major-key pieces usually do move from tonic to dominant in this way. If you pause the recording at the end of section A, the music sounds 'open', mainly because it is away from the home key. In major-key pieces it was common to touch on minor key(s) for contrast early in the B section, and Pachelbel does this very briefly (at about 4'10", if you're listening to FBC: 3).

> It may *sound* to those with absolute pitch as if FBC: 3 is in the keys of D♭ major and A♭ major. In this recording the instruments are tuned down, because when Pachelbel played a D, he heard a sound closer to our present-day D♭ than to our present-day D♮.

Bach's Air in D (FBC: 2) is also in binary form, but much more extended. Can you hear the AABB structure? Note that the repeats of A and B are ornamented in some performances, but this does not affect the overall form. Bach, like Pachelbel, ends section A in the dominant, which was usual in major-key pieces. However, if section A is short, the composer sometimes stays in the tonic key, but ends on chord V, with an imperfect cadence (as in the Allemanda from Corelli's Sonata Op. 2 No. 4,* WEM 2: 21). The final chord (V in the tonic) is the same as I in the dominant, but the effect is different – we end *on* the dominant *chord* rather than *in* the dominant *key*. Does Bach visit any minor keys in section B in his Air?

*The abbreviation 'Op.' is short for 'Opus', Latin for 'work'. Baroque composers gave opus numbers to *published sets* of pieces, generally sonatas and concertos.

Binary-form pieces which begin in a minor key often have section A ending in the dominant key. But composers sometimes ended section A in the relative major. In his Orchestral Suite No 2 in B minor, Bach ended section A of the light final movement (Badinerie) in F♯ minor (dominant of B minor), but section A of the first Bourrée in D major (relative major).

Rondeau form

As the name suggests, in a rondeau an opening passage in the tonic key keeps coming round – the most common pattern being ABACA (or, with repeats, AABACAA). The A section is the refrain or *rondeau*, the non-A passages are episodes or *couplets* (French: pronounced 'cooplay'). The rondeau originated in France and was at first the name of a medieval song with (as songs tend to have) a repeating pattern; repetition is all the medieval and Baroque rondeaux have in common. This French spelling was generally used by Baroque composers; later composers (in the Classical period) preferred 'rondo' (Italian). A Baroque rondeau and a Classical rondo are broadly similar in structure.

Charpentier's *Te Deum* Prelude is a rondeau (FBC: 1). Section A opens boldly with a melody for the trumpet based around a broken chord of D major, and with plenty of dotted rhythms (often associated in French Baroque music with dignity and solemnity). There is much repetition:

A (twice)	8 bars	D major
B	8 bars	D major – B minor – A major
A	8 bars	D major
C	8 bars	D major – B minor – E major – A major
A (twice)	8 bars	D major

On paper all this repetition of A looks uninteresting, as does the constant use of eight-bar sections, but the music works perfectly well in practice. It would have sounded highly effective in its context as a grand introduction to an extended piece of church music for an important occasion. Audiences and patrons – like many people nowadays – no doubt appreciated simple, fairly repetitive structures. Also, because most composers wrote vast amounts of music as part of their employment, they were more or less forced to adopt such labour-saving methods. Don't forget that before the age of recording, you couldn't hit pause buttons or repeat passages, so repetition in the piece helped audiences not to lose the plot.

Other simple rondeaux include two by Purcell (from *The Fairy Queen* and from *Abdelazar*) and Jeremiah Clarke's *The Prince of Denmark's March* (now often known as 'Trumpet Voluntary'), FBC: 10–12. Each, like Charpentier's, follows an AABACAA pattern. Listen for changes of key in each case. How far do the episodes re-use material from the refrain? Consider the opening melodic shape of B in the *Abdelazar* rondeau, for example.

Ritornello form

Many late-Baroque movements, especially from concertos, are in ritornello form. This is similar to rondeau but more sophisticated. An opening passage, itself often called 'ritornello' (Italian: 'a little return', meaning 'refrain'), is heard on two or more occasions – not always in the same key, and not necessarily in full, with other passages in between. These 'in-between' passages, sometimes much longer than the ritornellos, are called 'episodes', and are often for fewer instruments.

A ritornello can also be an instrumental passage within a vocal item. The ritornello in Lully's 'Ritournelle et récit de la fortune' from his *Ballet d'Alcidiane et Polexandre* (WEM 2: 11) appears three times, in the same key. The 'ritor[nello]' which ends Dido's lament in Purcell's *Dido and Aeneas* is heard only once (WEM 2: 12 / DMBE 1: 19).

Listen to the first movement of Vivaldi's Flute Concerto in D major, Op 10, no 3 (DMBE 2: 1). There are four ritornellos, the first and last in the tonic key, with three episodes. The first episode, with its rapid alternation of two notes and its trills helped to suggest the work's nickname *Il gardellino* (Italian: 'the goldfinch').

12. INSTRUMENTS AND VOICES

Both before and during the Baroque period, much instrumental music was never written down and is therefore unknown to us – especially music for players working outside the courtly and concert traditions, such as English 'waits', the minstrels employed by a town.

In terms of the classical 'written-down' tradition, instrumental music was much more important and plentiful in the Baroque period than it had been previously, when the majority of music was vocal. Improved instrument technology helped, and increasingly allowed and encouraged composers to develop genuinely instrumental ways of writing. You can tell immediately that Vivaldi's concertos *The Four Seasons* (Op. 8, Nos. 1–4) are written for instruments; on the other hand, some Renaissance-style music for instruments is much more vocal in character, for example Anthony Holborne's Pavan *The Image of Melancholy.* * But Vivaldi was not just composing for any instruments; he was quite specifically writing for strings. When music fits particular types of instruments, we say that the writing is *idiomatic*.

> *Some Renaissance music was actually designed to be sung *or* played!

It shouldn't surprise us that not much Baroque music was for voices only, given the importance of the new (instrumental) basso continuo principle. Previously, as we've seen, much Renaissance music *was* for voices only – although sometimes instruments may have doubled the voices. In fact instruments and voices could even have independent parts, notably in English ayres (songs for voice with lute accompaniment) by John Dowland (1563–1626), such as *Flow My Tears*, and in some anthems (for example Gibbons's *This is the Record of John*). But it was not until the early Baroque that the writing of independent parts for voices and instruments became a regular thing.

Instruments

Most of the instruments widely used in the Baroque period are direct forerunners of modern ones. But note that word 'forerunners': Baroque instruments were not identical in construction and sound to modern ones – some instruments familiar today (e.g. pianos and clarinets) were still evolving and sounded notably different. Others (e.g. saxophones) were unknown in Baroque times. Try to listen to some recordings which use 'period instruments' to get as close as possible to what 17th- and 18th-century listeners would have heard (FBC features period instruments). 'Period instruments' are either surviving Baroque instruments, or (more usually, especially in the case of winds) modern copies.

A selection of the instruments described in a late-Baroque Spanish treatise

The first violins, violas and cellos were made in Italy in the late 16th century (the early history of the double bass is less clear). For a time these 'violin family' instruments existed alongside the viol family, but gradually overtook them in popularity. The Baroque bow was straight or arch-shaped rather than inward-curving as today, and the bridge was slightly lower and its curve shallower, so that multiple stopping was easier. The neck bent back at a slighter angle and, together with the lower bridge, this put the strings at a lower tension, so that the sound was less powerful.

Viols (WEM 2: 16) normally had six strings, instead of four like members of the violin family, and were easier to play in tune because, like lutes and guitars, they had frets. Their sloping shoulders and flat backs distinguish them from the violin family (but link them to the double bass which retains these features). All three main types – treble, tenor and bass – were held on or against the leg; no viols were held under the chin like violins and violas.

Lutes, with their rounded backs, look like pears sliced vertically in two. They were at their most popular in the 16th century, but in Germany lute music was written right through to Bach's time. An archlute is a large lute with additional bass strings. A theorbo (or chittarone) is another type of large lute. Both were sometimes used as continuo instruments. Guitars became increasingly popular in southern Europe at the expense of lutes (which were harder to play). They were fashionable at the court of Louis XIV of France.

An archlute looks and sounds much like a theorbo; few people other than specialists can tell the difference (DMBE 1: 11 is for two theorbos and viols).

Recorders were widely used throughout the Baroque period (they fell out of favour after that, coming back into fashion in the 20th century, both in the classroom and in professional performances of Renaissance and Baroque music). There were several sizes, but F alto (treble) recorders were most common in the Baroque period. Bach is thought to have wanted treble recorders in his *Brandenburg* Concerto No. 4 – he asked (in Italian) for 'due Flauti d'Echo' ('two echo flutes').

Early and Late Baroque recorders

A flute, as in Bach's *Brandenburg* Concerto No. 5, was normally made of wood with finger holes and just one key for a hard-to-reach bass note. It lacked some of the brilliance of a modern metal flute and could not go so high, and was held sideways (unlike a recorder, which was end-blown). A flute was called 'flauto traverso' or just 'traversa' in Italian ('flauto' on its own meant 'recorder').

An oboe player, then as now, produced the sound by blowing between two reeds. The Baroque oboe (with fewer keys than the modern instrument) developed in the 17th century from the shawm, a more powerful, even raucous (and therefore often outdoor) instrument. In some Baroque music, oboes doubled (i.e. played the same parts as) violins, but they sometimes had solo roles as in concertos by Tomaso Albinoni (1671–1751). Bassoons are larger double-reed instruments than oboes. Usually they were part of the continuo, doubling the cellos, but Vivaldi wrote nearly 40 bassoon concertos.

Trumpets were often connected with royal and military ceremonies and were therefore regarded as special. They had no valves, and different notes were obtained simply by the player using different lip pressures – early brass instruments without the valves are called 'natural' (e.g. natural trumpet, natural horn). The *clarino* register was spectacularly high and bright – as in Bach's *Brandenburg* Concerto No. 2 (DMBE 2: 6 has the third movement).

Trombones were much favoured in Venice in the early 1600s, especially in ceremonial music for performance in church. Baroque trombones were less powerful than modern ones, and could be more successfully combined with softer instruments. To distinguish modern from Baroque instruments, the latter are conventionally called 'sackbutts' (alternative spelling 'sackbuts').

Horns are to be found in some late Baroque music (notably Bach's *Brandenburg* Concerto No. 1, which includes one called *corno da caccia* – Italian for 'hunting horn'). The *corno da caccia* had the circular shape of the modern horn, but was without valves, and had a lighter and brighter sound. It was much used in the high register.

Four *corni da caccia*

Timpani (or kettledrums) are used in some Baroque music, usually with trumpets where a grand ceremonial effect is required.

Harpsichords are keyboard instruments with strings which are mechanically plucked when the keys are pressed. Baroque harpsichords varied considerably in tone and construction from one country to another.

Clavichords are keyboard instruments with strings which are hit by 'tangents' when the keys, which have a seesaw action, are pressed. In the Baroque period clavichords were used mainly in Germany. Their quiet sound made them unsuitable for public occasions, but ideal for domestic music-making. Unlike harpsichords, they were touch-sensitive. In this way, and in the 'hammer' sound production, they are like modern pianos.

Organs varied greatly in size, tone and construction. German organs usually had two or more manuals (keyboards for the hands) and pedals (a keyboard for the feet). English organs normally had no pedals and rarely more than one manual.

Instrumental groupings

In the early 17th century, composers tended to use whatever instruments happened to be available. Perhaps this explains, for example, what may seem to 21st-century listeners a rather odd collection of instruments in Giovanni Gabrieli's *Sonata pian' e forte* (DMBE 1: 6 / WEM 2: 6): six trombones, one cornett and one viola.

As time went on, various standard instrumental groupings (sometimes different from those used in more recent times) came into use. These were mainly of stringed instruments, partly because strings were more versatile and reliable than early wind instruments. But also in the late 17th century many influential people (including Charles II of England) were impressed by the string bands which Lully directed at the court of Louis XIV – in particular the *Grande Bande* (French: 'large band'), which was also known as the *Vingt-quatre Violons du Roi* (French: 'the king's 24 violins').* The 'large band' had six violins to play the melody and six bass violins (like cellos but slightly bigger) on the bass part. The other players divided into three groups of four to take the middle parts. They played instruments larger than violins but smaller than bass violins – in effect small, medium-sized and large violas. Sometimes the violin and bass parts were doubled by oboes and/or bassoons. Trumpets and timpani, played by musicians who worked with the cavalry, were also sometimes added.

*The *Vingt-quatre Violons* were sometimes supplemented by other court musicians, notably from the *Douze Grands Hautbois du Roi* (a band of twelve players consisting of ten oboes and two bassoons).

The Italians later preferred the layout which is still at the heart of the modern orchestra, with two sets of violins ('firsts' and 'seconds'), violas and cellos. It's uncertain where and when double basses (doubling the cello part an octave lower) became regular members of the orchestra.

Whereas some present-day orchestras are large, with up to 100 players, including 50 or more string players and lots of woodwind, brass and percussion, Baroque orchestras were usually quite small, both in overall numbers of players and types of instruments, for example the 24 members of Louis XIV's *Vingt-quatre Violons*. In Italy, Corelli some-times worked with 40 or more players – even occasionally with 70.

Voices

Most choirs generally, as now, sang in four parts. Like cathedral choirs today, church choirs had men and boys, usually with boys (trebles) singing the top part and with men singing the alto or countertenor, tenor and bass parts.* Women sang in opera and some other kinds of secular (non-church) music, as a rule taking soprano and alto parts while men sang tenor and bass.

*Men who sang alto or countertenor parts were either high tenors or sang *falsetto* (using a special high register most familiar to many people from the work of some pop singers, including Barry Gibb of the Bee Gees). The word 'countertenor' is widely used for any adult male voice higher than ordinary tenor, but falsettists are often termed male altos.

In opera (especially Italian opera), solo parts of soprano range were sometimes sung by *castrati*, who were extremely popular at the time; their boyish unbroken range was combined with adult power and projection. Among the most famous were Farinelli (born Carlo Broschi) and Senesino (born Francesco Bernardi). Today, these parts are sometimes sung by women, sometimes by countertenors. Farinelli (1705–1782) was the subject of a French film *Farinelli* (1994, director Gérard Corbiau). It's not always histori-cally accurate, but good use is made of music from Farinelli's own time. The filmmakers combined elements from the voices of two singers, a countertenor and a soprano, to achieve an approximation to Farinelli's range and vocal power.

13. SUITES

The next six chapters provide a brief review of Baroque music by investigating major genres. We begin with three chapters on instrumental music, partly because this is the way into Baroque music for so many people, and where we started back in Chapter 2. We shall deal in turn with suites, sonatas and concertos.

A suite is a group of dances in the same key, sometimes with one or more movements that are not dances. The suite reached its peak in the late Baroque. Dances had sometimes been grouped in the Renaissance – usually in pairs (especially pavan and galliard). Well-known post-Baroque suites include Tchaikovsky's *Nutcracker* Suite, a selection from the ballet of the same name (1892).

Dance music for playing and listening

Much dance music was composed for the stage in the Baroque period, above all in France with its flourishing tradition of ballet. FBC: 17 has Rameau's 'Menuet tendre en rondeau', or 'Tender minuet in rondeau form', from his opera *Dardanus*, 1739.

But many Baroque pieces with dance titles were composed for playing and listening. They are often more elaborate than music for dancing, but can still be called 'dances' because they borrow certain dance features. These may include time signature, tempo, characteristic rhythm patterns, and 'regular' two- and four-bar phrases. For example, Pachelbel's Gigue in D (FBC: 3, beginning at 3'24") is in quick $\frac{12}{8}$ time.

Dances are generally in binary form. However, composers sometimes extended their work in one of the following ways:

■ Two dances of the same kind (both binary) appear in the order first dance, second dance, first dance repeated, producing a kind of ternary (ABA) structure. This happens for example with the two gavottes in Bach's Orchestral Suite No 3 in D. This version of ternary later became the Classical 'minuet and trio' form, where two minuets (the second entitled trio) were played in the order minuet, trio, minuet. The minuet was the only Baroque dance still widely used in the Classical period; it formed an important connecting link from suite to symphony, and developed into the scherzo – a faster type of movement, often with a strong element of humour or surprise – as used through the Romantic period and beyond.

■ Two versions of a single dance are given, the first 'plain', the second (a 'double' – pronounced the French way, 'doobluh') with much ornamentation added. Some modern performers play the plain dance complete, with both sections repeated (AABB) and then the double similarly (AvAvBvBv, with v meaning 'varied'). A different approach (AAvBBv) is possible. Baroque performers may sometimes have played either the plain dance or the double, not both. The musical example below shows the start of the Sarabande from Bach's English Suite No. 6 in D minor, with its double. As in many other doubles, the melody is ornamented, while the bass remains the same.

J S Bach, Sarabande and Double from English Suite No. 6 in D minor (BWV 811)

In the Double, Bach embellished the original sarabande, not generally with conventional signs for ornaments such as trills and mordents, but with small fully-notated additions.* Behind these added notes there is the same mostly chordal texture, but the little motifs passing between the various parts give the impression that you're listening to a more contrapuntal texture (concerning counterpoint, see Chapter 9) than is really the case. At times the music sounds almost as if it is for lute, where you have to 'fake' counterpoint in this way rather than playing strictly in the same number of parts throughout. This lute-based style, much used in 17th-century France, gradually spread to keyboard writing. Nowadays the term *style brisé* is often used (pronounced 'steel breezay').

*Note however, that Bach used ornament signs when he wished: for example, see those in bar 2 of the original sarabande. Some French keyboard composers, notably François Couperin, provided many such ornaments, or *agréments*, as for instance in his Sarabande *Les Sentiments* ('Feelings', DMBE 2: 12).

The structure of a Baroque suite

There is no *fixed* pattern of movements. But many late Baroque suites include the following four dances, in this order:

Allemande	usually moderate speed or fairly slow, in $\frac{4}{4}$ time, with a short upbeat and plenty of gentle semiquaver movement
Courante	quick or fairly quick, usually in $\frac{3}{2}$ or $\frac{3}{4}$
Sarabande	slow triple time, usually $\frac{3}{4}$, often with the second beat of the bar emphasised
Gigue	quick and lively, usually in a compound time such as $\frac{12}{8}$

Note that the speed of a dance isn't usually indicated by the composer. Players were guided by the title and the 'feel' of the music. For further detail on the character of different dance types, see, for example D. Bowman, *Rhinegold Dictionary of Music in Sound* (Rhinegold, 2002).

There are often additional dances, especially between the sarabande and gigue. Whereas the allemande, courante, sarabande and gigue had all developed before the Baroque period, the additional dances (such as minuets and gavottes) were mainly of 17th-century French origin. In operas and ballets Lully and Rameau often focused on these 'modern' types of dances.

Some suites, including Bach's English Suites and Partitas for keyboard, begin with a prelude or other kind of non-dance movement. Some include such a movement (often an Air) later on. Partitas are suites by a different name: composers weren't consistent in their use of titles. Some works called 'sonata' or 'sonata da camera' are also similar to suites (see Chapter 14). The opening movement of a suite could also be called an 'overture': see page 69 for an explanation of this borrowing from opera and ballet practice.

Bach's English and French Suites and Partitas

For many people, Bach's English and French Suites and Partitas for keyboard – six in each set – mark the high point of the Baroque suite. The Partitas were published one at a time (1726–1731); the French Suites (which Bach didn't publish) probably date from the early 1720s, the English Suites from slightly earlier. It's not clear how the English and French Suites got their names. Bach follows the basic four-movement scheme outlined above, but there's much variety in his choice of additional dances, and in the character of the non-dance movements which head the English Suites and Partitas. In the Orchestral Suites Bach chose mainly 'modern' dances – although No. 1 does have a courante, No. 2 a sarabande, and No. 3 a gigue.

There is also some variety within each category of dance. For example, the courante can be in French style, in $\frac{3}{2}$ time, or can be a quicker Italian *corrente* in $\frac{3}{4}$ ('courante' is the French for 'running'; 'corrente' is the Italian). The courante in the French Suite No. 1 in D minor is a French courante; Suite No. 5 in G has an Italian-style movement. Sometimes in editions of Bach's music both types are labelled 'courante'. There are correntes in some of Corelli's trio sonatas (e.g. Op. 2 No. 2 in D minor): they are less scalic (less running) than Bach's, but lighter and more dance-like.

The Baroque gigue is a descendant of the jig, a folk dance from the British Isles, which both the French and the Italians house-trained in the 17th century. Lully's gigues often use imitation, quite long phrases of irregular length, and begin with a two-note upbeat (consisting of a short note and a longer note). A giga by Corelli ('giga' is the Italian version of the word 'gigue') tends to have a clearer, more regular phrase structure, and to be simpler in texture (see, for example, the last movement of the violin sonata Op. 5 No. 10 in F).

By the early 18th century the gigue and giga had cross-fertilised. Bach utilised Italian-style rhythms, but with imitation in the French manner; however a few of his gigues do have characteristically French rhythms:

J. S. Bach, Gigue from French Suite No. 2 in C minor (BWV 813)

14. SONATAS

A sonata is usually:

- An instrumental piece
- For one or a small number of instruments
- In three or more movements.

In many Baroque sonatas (and concertos) all movements are in the same key, as in suites. In the early 18th century this began to change, and we find (as in Classical and later works) that one movement is in a different, closely related, key (see for example Bach's organ sonatas). However, the first and last movements still had to be in the same key – this was not so with operas, oratorios and cantatas where composers were happy with looser overall key schemes.

How sonatas originated

The word 'sonata' (Italian for 'played' or 'sounded') was originally vague: it meant a piece that you played as opposed to a piece that you sang, for example, Giovanni Gabrieli's *Sonata pian' e forte* (WEM 2: 6 / DMBE 1: 6).

It is all the more odd, therefore, that sonatas as we now understand them have their roots in vocal music. In the 16th century some French composers wrote secular (non-church) pieces for voices called *chansons* (literally 'songs'). Italian composers would sometimes arrange a chanson for instruments and call it *canzone francese* ('French song') or *canzone*. (A canzone is now usually called a *canzona* with an a.) Other names for these arrangements were *canzone da sonare* ('song for playing') or, from the 1580s, just sonata ('played').

Sections and movements

The earliest sonatas had one movement, with (like some chansons and canzonas) contrasting sections. As time went on, sections became extended and more separate. In other words, sections became movements.

A movement is a piece within a piece. Unlike a section, it's usually complete in itself, and can be played on its own. However, some Baroque slow movements are not like this, but end with a 'Phrygian' cadence as a special way of leading straight into a final quick movement. A Phrygian cadence is a type of imperfect cadence in a minor key, with chords IVb and V. The Adagio in Corelli's Sonata Op. 2 No. 4 has a Phrygian cadence in E minor, to lead into an E minor giga. (WEM 2: 21, however, ends with the Adagio – leaving us high and dry!) In the early 18th century you could end a movement with a Phrygian cadence in one key and then start the next movement in the *relative major* – as in Bach's Organ Sonata No. 5 (second movement: A minor; third movement: C major).

Some aspects of the Baroque sonata were variable:

- There was no fixed *number* of movements
- There was no fixed *pattern* of movements.

Nevertheless, it was not chaos. Baroque sonatas often had four movements, and composers contrasted slow and quick, almost always finishing with a quick movement. Many of Corelli's trio sonatas, for example, have a four-movement S–Q–S–Q ('S' for 'slow', 'Q' for 'quick') pattern. However, Bach (perhaps influenced by Vivaldi) preferred the pattern Q–S–Q in his organ sonatas. Classical and later composers likewise usually started with a quick movement. This was often in 'sonata form', a type of musical form referred to in most dictionary articles on sonata but developed *after* the Baroque period.

Arcangelo Corelli

Types of sonata: church and chamber

A sonata without dance titles and with movement(s) in contrapuntal style was sometimes called a *sonata da chiesa* ('church sonata'), because it was for use in church services as well as elsewhere – sonatas or separate movement(s) would probably be played at points where there would otherwise be silence in the service. Corelli's Op. 1 and Op. 3 trio sonatas are of the 'church' type, although the composer didn't actually call them *sonate da chiesa* (*sonate* = plural of *sonata*). Players would know anyway – partly because Corelli asked for an organ on the continuo part.

A sonata consisting of movements with dance titles in binary form was sometimes termed a *sonata da camera* ('chamber sonata'): it was for entertainment at home or in public, not for use in church as a *sonata da camera* was. A 'chamber', incidentally, is a room in a house or palace, which could be small or large – the word didn't refer to a public concert hall.

A *sonata da camera* can be thought of as an Italian version of the suite; Corelli published the 12 trio sonatas of Op. 2 as *sonate da camera*, with harpsichord not organ on the continuo part. His Op. 2 No. 4 has a slow prelude, an allemanda, a two-section slow movement (short Grave and longer Adagio), and a giga. The common S–Q–S–Q movement pattern underlies this. WEM 2: 21 has the Q–S part of this (the allemanda and two-section slow movement). Interestingly, Corelli no longer thought it necessary to label his Op. 4 chamber sonatas *sonate da camera* – it was obvious what they were. As time went on, the distinction between church and chamber sonatas became increasingly blurred.

Sonatas and instruments

Sonatas are mainly composed for a single instrument (usually keyboard), for a melody instrument (commonly violin) and continuo, or for two violins and continuo.

Sonatas for one instrument

Sonatas for keyboard (usually harpsichord) belong to the later Baroque. Domenico Scarlatti (1685–1757, DMBE 1: 3 and 2: 3, 4) composed hundreds; some were published as *essercizi* ('exercises'). His sonatas have only one movement, but were often paired to make two-movement works. A few were fairly simple pieces for amateurs, but others are technically very challenging, with crossing of hands and wide leaps – Scarlatti himself was a virtuoso keyboard player.* There are echoes of Spanish guitar and folk music: Scarlatti spent some years in Spain, the country which ruled Naples at the time of his birth (Naples is now of course part of Italy).

*A virtuoso is a performer with exceptional technical skill.

Harmony was so important to Baroque composers that they wrote few sonatas for a single melody instrument; but Bach was thinking just as much as usual about harmony in his sonatas for unaccompanied violin (the outstanding examples of their kind – DMBE 1: 2 has the first movement of Sonata No. 1). In particular, he uses a lot of multiple stopping and is even able to suggest the separate voices of a fugue in the second movement of each sonata.

Sonatas for melody instrument and continuo

Where there was one instrument and continuo, the composer wrote down just two parts, the solo part and the bass. (Remember that a keyboard or lute player improvised an accompaniment, so that more than two parts were actually heard.) But often you had three performers – the soloist, a keyboard or lute player, and someone doubling the bass part on (for example) a cello. There wasn't *always* a bass player – the texture was complete anyway.

The violin was the favourite solo instrument. Violin sonatas from the 1610s and 1620s by Biagio Marini (c. 1595–1665) are among the earliest. Corelli, Vivaldi and Handel were important later composers for the violin. (Note that a sonata for violin and continuo is often called a 'violin sonata'; to avoid misunderstanding, we usually say that sonatas for violin only, such as Bach's, are 'for unaccompanied violin'.)

Sonatas were written for other instruments apart from violin, notably recorder, flute or oboe. Handel's Sonata Op. 1 No. 4 in A minor is for recorder, for example, and his Op. 1 No. 8 in C minor is for oboe.

Composers sometimes gave a choice of instrument. For instance, Francesco Maria Veracini (1690–1768) published sonatas for violin *or* recorder – a shrewd commercial move. But this was not the usual way: composers were increasingly keen to write idiomatically. Bach's sonatas for unaccompanied violin are very definitely violin music. So are Corelli's sonatas (Op. 5). Look at the second vivace from Sonata No. 5, below. Corelli uses multiple stopping, and also frequently visits G below middle C – something else not possible for flutes, recorders and oboes but a favourite with violin composers for its distinctive sound quality or timbre.

Corelli, Sonata in G minor, Op. 5 No. 5, fourth movement: Vivace

Sonatas for keyboard and melody instrument

In a few sonatas, the composer gave the keyboard player a fully written out part, so that he partnered rather than just accompanied the melody instrument. The most important are Bach's six sonatas for keyboard and violin (BWV 1014–1019), which were probably composed before 1725. In their basic method (rather than in musical style) they point ahead to Classical sonatas such as Mozart's for keyboard and violin.

Trio sonatas

Trio sonatas have *two* solo parts plus basso continuo. Corelli, Purcell and Handel composed many fine examples. The term 'trio sonata' is modern: Corelli, for example, called his trio sonatas *sonate a tre* ('sonatas in three parts'). The word 'trio' implies three players, but often a trio sonata involved *four* people – the continuo part being played by two of them. Like most trio sonatas, Corelli's Op. 2 No. 4 has two violins. The third part is for 'violone' (probably bass violin or cello) and 'cembalo' (harpsichord). The example below shows the beginning and ending of the allemande (WEM 2: 21).

Corelli, Sonata in E minor, Op. 2 No. 4, second movement: Allemanda

The two violins in a trio sonata are usually similar in range and musical interest, unlike the first and second violins in a string quartet or an orchestra, where the first has a higher and more prominent part than the second. Not surprisingly therefore, the violin parts in a trio sonata frequently cross, as in bar 3 of musical example (a) above. The intertwining violins are often a long way above the bass, with the keyboard or lute player filling in the gap. Suspensions are a feature of the style (there are some figured '7 6' in example (b) above). Suspensions are accented dissonances much loved by Baroque composers for their ability to spice up the harmony. For more information, see *AS Music Harmony Workbook* (Rhinegold, 2008), pages 58–60.

15. CONCERTOS

Most concertos composed after the Baroque period are big three-movement works for solo instrument and large orchestra, with very showy solo parts (for example, Romantic piano concertos by Grieg and Tchaikovsky). In the Baroque period, however, a concerto could mean any of the following:

- A work for voices and instruments, as in early Baroque church music (see Chapter 8)
- A concerto grosso for three or more soloists (making up the 'concertino') plus supporting players (the 'ripieno') and continuo
- A solo concerto for single soloist, plus ripieno and continuo
- A double concerto for two soloists, plus ripieno and continuo
- An orchestral concerto, or concerto-sinfonia, for orchestra only, although some sections may be more elaborate than others.

Concertos involve *contrast* – between different groups of performers, and/or between technically difficult parts for soloists and simpler parts for others. Contrast between different groupings is already clear in some early 17th-century music, including Gabrieli's *Sonata pian' e forte* (WEM 2: 6 / DMBE 1: 6). This begins with two *pian'* (*piano* = quiet) sections, for 'Coro 1' (cornett and trombones 1–3), and 'Coro 2' (viola and trombones 4–6). Then everyone plays together *forte* (= loud). Similar contrasts follow.

Concerti grossi: Corelli, Handel and Vivaldi

Corelli's 12 Concerti grossi Op. 6 were among the earliest. Corelli took his trio sonata grouping (two violins and cello) as the concertino, and added other strings (including a viola part) as the ripieno. He may have expected one keyboard instrument to play with the concertino and another with the ripieno – it's not quite clear. He would probably have been happy with just one keyboard if only one was available. The concertino parts were not as a rule more elaborate than the others, but they were more important. They were heard more or less throughout, whereas the ripieno played only from time to time (often just doubling the concertino). The ripieno parts were optional (presumably to encourage performances where few players were available); but if you miss them out there's no concertino part to double the ripieno viola part. However, provided you have a keyboard or lute player the harmony *is* complete. Contrasts arose from the changes of texture caused by the changes in numbers of players. These in turn resulted in different dynamics – the music was louder when the ripieno played than when it didn't (compare Gabrieli's *Sonata pian' e forte*).

You can hear these contrasts clearly in, for example, the 'Christmas' Concerto Op. 6 No. 8 in G minor, in the energetic first allegro, and also in the lovely pastorale (WEM 2: 23 / DMBE 1: 20) which typically is in $\frac{12}{8}$ time, moderate in speed and gentle in character; the long held notes suggest the drones of rustic bagpipes.* It was an optional concluding movement, for performance in church on Christmas Eve, intended to make listeners think of the shepherds in the fields outside Bethlehem in the Christmas story (Handel's 'Pastoral symphony' from *Messiah*, Act 1, depicts the same scene).

> *The title is connected with 'pastore' (Italian for 'shepherd'), and with 'pastoral', another word for rural in English).

Corelli's first seven concertos (Op. 6 Nos. 1–7) were also suitable for church, (although probably they were also performed elsewhere). They are the concerto equivalents of the church sonata (*sonata da chiesa*), and you could describe each as a church concerto or *concerto da chiesa,* although Corelli himself didn't bother to. There's no fixed number of movements, but the familiar S–Q–S–Q pattern underlies some of Corelli's more extended arrangements. Concertos 9–12 include dance movements, and each could be called a chamber concerto or *concerto da camera* (No. 11, for example, has preludio, allemanda, adagio, sarabanda and giga).

Handel's work includes six *Concerti grossi* Op. 3 (published 1734), and 12 Grand Concertos Op. 6 (1740), 'Grand Concertos' being Handel's translation of 'concerti grossi'. He, like Corelli, uses a concertino of two violins and cello, and avoids showy passages for them. But the orchestra isn't limited to doubling the soloists – for example, there's a dialogue between concertino and ripieno at the start of Op. 6 No. 1. Sometimes, however, as in the whole of Op. 6 No. 7, the ripieno doubles the concertino so that the concertino players have no independent parts. This is more typical of an orchestral concerto than of a concerto grosso. Some movements from other concertos are in the orchestral concerto style: listen for example to DMBE 1: 1 and 2: 21.

Altogether Handel's concerti grossi are very varied: for example the fourth movement of Op. 6 No. 6 has solo passages for one violin, and is therefore in the style of a solo concerto. There is no standard pattern of movements. A few concertos have one or more dance movements. Op. 6 No. 8, for example, begins with an allemande, includes a siciliana* and ends with an untitled dance-like movement in $\frac{12}{8}$. The other movements are not in dance styles. Handel's concertos, and movements from them, were sometimes played between the acts of oratorios – there's no reason to believe that they were performed in church. Handel didn't use the terms *chiesa* and *camera,* incidentally: the old distinction had broken down by the time he wrote his concertos.

> *A type of instrumental or vocal movement often used to suggest pastoral scenes. Normally fairly slow and in a lilting compound time.

Vivaldi wrote about 30 concerti grossi and more than ten times as many solo concertos. His Concerto Op. 3 No. 2 in G minor has two solo violins and cello, but generally he experimented with different combinations of instruments, often including wind instruments. He preferred a three-movement pattern (Q–S–Q), which Bach also adopted.

Caricature of Antonio Vivaldi c. 1723

Bach's Brandenburg concertos

J. S. Bach's six *Brandenburg* concertos are exceptionally fine. These were dedicated to the Margrave of Brandenburg, a German aristocrat, who seems not to have had suitable players to perform them. They include three magnificent concerti grossi – Nos. 2 (DMBE 2: 6 has the 3rd movement), 4 and 5 – each with a different concertino. However, in each work one soloist takes the lead. So instead of the usual two 'layers' (concertino plus ripieno) there are three, with leading soloist, other soloists (see below) plus ripieno. In effect Bach has blended the concerto grosso and the solo concerto; it was his special gift to draw together different styles or genres and make something greater out of their union than anyone had ever made out of them separately.

No. 2	trumpet	violin, recorder, oboe	ripieno
No. 4	violin	two recorders	ripieno
No. 5	harpsichord	violin, flute	ripieno

Brandenburg No. 5 was probably the first concerto ever to include a solo keyboard instrument. The harpsichord part (for Bach himself to play?) is challenging and varied. There is an unaccompanied display passage near the end of the first movement, whereas in the ritornellos the player improvises an accompaniment from the basso continuo part. The violinist and flautist don't have outstandingly difficult parts, but still enjoy much more of the limelight than Corelli's or Handel's soloists. The unaccompanied display passage mentioned above is marked *'cembalo solo senza stromenti'* ('harpsichord solo without instruments'), but is usually referred to nowadays as a cadenza (a term of Baroque origin derived from the Italian for 'cadence', and meaning a showy solo passage, often improvised, near the end of a section or movement).

The ritornellos are for strings plus continuo (the solo violin doubling the ripieno violins – there's just one ripieno violin part, not firsts and seconds as usual). The soloists play in the other sections ('episodes') with light string accompaniment. This accompaniment borrows from the ritornello, so that the ritornello and episodes are subtly linked.

Brandenburg Concertos Nos. 1, 3 and 6 are not strictly concerti grossi. No. 1 is a kind of orchestral concerto for strings, oboes and horns, with interesting contrasts of scoring between sections and movements. The strings include a solo part for a small kind of violin known as a *violino piccolo* which was tuned higher than an ordinary one and on which it was easier to play high notes; the sound would have carried well over that of the other strings. Concertos 3 and 6 use only strings, but in highly original ways. No. 3 has three trios (number symbolism always fascinated Bach – see page 96 for more on this) of strings – violins, violas and cellos – plus continuo. Each group takes the lead in turn. No. 6 has an unusually dark timbre. There are no violins: two solo violas are supported by two viols (the viola da gamba is similar in range to the cello, but with a lighter, reedier sound), cello, double bass and continuo.

Solo and double concertos

The solo concerto developed later than the concerto grosso. One important early composer was Giuseppe Torelli (1658–1709). The third movement of Concerto Op. 8 No. 8 (published 1709), already has in simple form the kind of ritornello structure developed by later composers. In the three ritornellos the soloist plays with the first violins. In the two other sections his part is more elaborate than the ripieno parts, although it's not difficult by Romantic or 20th-century standards.

Torelli, Concerto Op. 8 No. 8, third movement

Corelli composed no solo concertos, but Vivaldi was fascinated by the new medium and produced well over 300. Many were for his own instrument, the violin. Other solo instruments included bassoon, cello, oboe, flute, recorder, and mandolin.

Vivaldi's best-known solo concertos are the four he composed for violin, known as *The Four Seasons*, Op. 8 Nos. 1–4, published in 1725. They are great favourites, partly because of how the composer depicts various characters and incidents, for example the storm in the third movement of No. 2 ('Summer'). Poems accompanying the musical score articulate what each concerto is meant to depict. This was unusual because very little Baroque instrumental music attempts to tell a story – such depiction became widespread only in the 19th century. However, Heinrich Biber (1644–1704) had already based his 'Mystery' or 'Rosary' violin sonatas (c. 1676) on a series of religious pictures.

The opening of 'Spring' shows how simple and direct many of Vivaldi's musical ideas were. The melody makes the key immediately clear by outlining the tonic chord. In fact Vivaldi is obsessed with chord I throughout the first four phrases (see the music example below). Bach was influenced by Vivaldi's clear definition of key through triad-shaped themes, for example in the opening E–G♯–B motif from his Violin Concerto in E.

Vivaldi, Concerto in E major, Op. 8 No. 1, *La primavera* ('Spring'), first movement

Handel 'invented' the organ concerto in the 1730s (see Chapter 20, pages 93–94), and composed more than a dozen, for performance with a small orchestra of strings (and sometimes oboes) between the acts of oratorios. He himself was the soloist, and sometimes improvised additional movements for organ only. Bach, though the leading composer for the organ, composed no organ concertos, but some large-scale solo works at times resemble concertos (see Chapter 20, page 95).

Bach composed two concertos for solo violin, and adapted both (and *Brandenburg Concerto No. 4*) as harpsichord concertos. The Concerto in D minor for two violins and strings is usually known as a 'double concerto'. Bach also adapted this, for two harpsichords and strings. His concerto for four harpsichords and strings is an arrangement of a concerto by Vivaldi for four violins and strings (Op. 3 No. 10). Bach probably performed it with three of his sons, perhaps for the Leipzig *Collegium Musicum* (Chapter 19, page 89). Vivaldi himself wrote some 40 or more double concertos (many for two violins).

16. OPERAS

We move on now to three chapters dealing with music that includes voices. Such vocal music can be divided into two main types – sacred (with religious words) and secular. We consider the principal genre of secular music – opera – in this chapter, because opera is where Baroque music really began, as explained in Chapter 8.

An opera is a large-scale dramatic work for singers and instrumentalists. In most operas there is music throughout, and all words are sung. However, some 18th-century operas (among them English ballad operas) included speech, and Purcell's semi-operas (for example *The Fairy Queen*) had both singing and speaking roles. Operas normally featured some instrumental music, chiefly at the beginning (the 'overture'), and there may be, as in many French operas, dances with instrumental accompaniment.

Monteverdi's *Orfeo*

The earliest opera that has really stood the test of time is Monteverdi's *Orfeo*, staged in 1607 at Mantua.

Orfeo is musically more ambitious and much more interesting than the operas of Peri and Caccini. Simple monody is still vital, but much of the vocal writing is more song-like, varied and expressive, with a clearer sense of form and structure and more arias, duets and ensembles. The plot concerns Orpheus, the legendary poet-musician, who was allowed to take his wife Euridice back from the underworld after her death, but didn't keep his promise not to look at her until they had both reached the world above. Euridice was snatched back into the underworld, and Orpheus was grief-stricken – but there was a *kind* of happy ending. With cruel irony, however, Monteverdi's own wife died shortly after the opera had been composed.

Title page from the 1609 printing of Monteverdi's *Orfeo*

A list in the published score (Venice, 1609 – second edition 1615) shows Monteverdi's instrumental resourcefulness, with his use of violins, viols, recorders, cornetts, trumpets, trombones, harp, chittarone, two harpsichords and three (small) organs. The handling of this assorted 'orchestra' is striking, not least in the lively opening toccata. (Monteverdi later made this into the opening movement of his *Vespers* (see DMBE 1: 7) by adding voices.) *Orfeo* was originally described as *favola in musica*, Italian for 'tale (or fable) in music'. In fact early and mid 17th-century Italian operas bore various names, including often *dramma per musica* ('drama through music'). *Opera*, an Italian word just meaning 'work', and therefore pretty vague, was not yet in standard use, but it is the obvious term for us to use today.

Opera in Venice

The earliest operas, including *Orfeo*, were sung in the palaces of the aristocracy, mainly in Florence, Mantua and Rome. In 1637 the first public staging of opera took place in Venice, and it was soon widely performed in theatres there, becoming a profitable business.

It was for Venice that Monteverdi composed one of the finest of all operas – *L'incoronazione di Poppea* ('The Coronation of Poppea', 1642). The text (or libretto) is based partly on history – Poppea was the wife of the Roman emperor Nero – and this is probably one reason why the characters come alive as human beings more than in the earliest operas on subjects from mythology.

Venice remained a major centre of opera after Monteverdi's death in 1643. His principal successors were Francesco Cavalli (1602–1676) and Antonio Cesti (1623–1669). Cavalli wrote more than 30 operas, among them *Xerse* and *Erismena* (1655). Cesti is most widely known for *Il pomo d'oro* ('The Golden Apple', 1668), a work of exceptional splendour first staged in Vienna.

Singers were becoming more and more the centre of attention – Cesti himself was a celebrated tenor. Partly as a result, composers increasingly concentrated on writing beautiful melodic arias that would also give singers opportunities for display. The Italian term *bel canto* ('beautiful singing') is sometimes applied to the style of mid 17th-century composers such as Cavalli and Cesti, in contrast to the more functional text-dominated style of the early Baroque.

Generally, music was now either melodious and elaborate (in arias) or plainer and more functional (in recitatives), though an in-between style called 'arioso' is sometimes found. Recitatives are the successors to the simpler forms of monody pioneered by Peri and Caccini. Composers set the words clearly and often rapidly with the aim of moving the dramatic action along.

Neapolitan opera

Opera became popular in many regions, including Naples (southern Italy, then ruled by Spain); in fact the word 'Neapolitan' in the heading above means 'of or from Naples'. Alessandro Scarlatti (father of Domenico Scarlatti, 1660–1725) helped to establish the type of Neapolitan opera which was dominant in the early 18th century, not only in Italy but in other countries apart from France. The international character of Neapolitan opera is proved by the fact that Handel, its most outstanding composer, was a German working in London. It may seem odd that Handel wrote operas for the English stage in an Italian style with Italian words. Opera can of course work as drama when people don't understand every word that's sung. But Handel's audiences also just liked listening to their favourite singers and to his music.

In the early 18th century Italian opera lost some of its spontaneity and became increasingly governed by rules and conventions. And whereas earlier operas had had lighter, comic scenes, these were now considered too frivolous for 'serious opera' (*opera seria*) and were dropped, leaving comic opera to evolve separately from the comic *intermezzi* ('interval' pieces) still allowed between the acts of serious opera. Giovanni Battista

Pergolesi (1710–1736) wrote a fine comic *intermezzo* called *La serva padrona* ('The serv-ant-girl as mistress') in 1733. The characters in comic opera are often 'ordinary' people rather than heroes and heroines from ancient Greek or Roman history or mythology.

In Neapolitan opera most scenes were divided into two very separate parts – recita-tive and aria. In the recitative you had action and simple clear projection of the text, in the aria there was reflection and a musically more elaborate and tuneful style. This division seems very artificial; after all, life is not like that – but then life doesn't contain flashbacks or close-ups either and that has never stopped film directors.

People not used to Neapolitan opera may also find it particularly strange that during an aria lasting for several minutes nothing much happens on the stage. In fact, composers usually kill any chance of dramatic development by ending their arias with a return to the words and music of the opening section. These and other apparently irrational conventions did provide clear structure, simplicity and order, however, and they were used sensitively by those who, like Handel, had a strong feeling for opera as drama.

Recitatives

Most recitatives were *secco* (Italian, 'dry'), with continuo accompaniment. Occasionally, for special effect, they were *accompagnato* or *stromentato*, with fuller accompaniment. (To understand the word *stromentato*, think of '[in]strument'.)

A *secco* recitative:

- ■ Has a $\frac{4}{4}$ or **C** time signature
- ■ Isn't obviously tuneful; the melody helps to project the words by reflecting the rhythm and pitch of the speaking voice

> It's easiest for English speakers to hear this in a recitative with English words, such as 'Behold, a Virgin shall conceive' (from Handel's oratorio *Messiah*, No. 8).

- ■ Often begins with a first-inversion (6/3) chord
- ■ Has a slower rate of chord change than most Baroque music, the harmony just *supporting* the voice
- ■ Ends with a tacked-on perfect cadence clearly separate from what's gone before; if the recitative is long, similar cadence(s) earlier on act like paragraph breaks
- ■ Often begins and ends in different keys, which can help in linking two arias.

Arias

Many arias in Neapolitan opera end by repeating the opening section. They are said to be in *da capo* form, which is a version of ternary (ABA) form. *Da capo* (Italian) means 'from the beginning', because at the end of the B section, the performers return to the start and work through the A section again. To start the A section, the orchestra usually has an introductory passage (ritornello), which returns at the end. In between, ideas from the ritornello may reappear in the voice or accompaniment. The B section provides contrast, notably through a different key. In the repeat of the A section the singer usually adds some improvised ornamentation. In some arias from Neapolitan opera the singer's first phrase stands on its own as a kind of announcement, helping to establish the 'affection' of the aria, as in the music example below, from a well-known aria by Handel.

Handel, 'Ombra mai fù' from *Serse* ('Xerxes'), Act I

'Ombra mai fù'* is not a *da capo* aria; Handel, the most important composer of Neapolitan opera, didn't use *da capo* form blindly for every aria, nor did he stick rigidly to the recitative-plus-aria pattern in every scene. Nevertheless he composed plenty of *da capo* arias. An example is Cleopatra's 'Tutto può donna vezzosa' ('A pretty woman can achieve anything') from *Giulio Cesare in Egitto* ('Julius Caesar in Egypt', 1724).

> *Strangely, instrumental arrangements of 'Ombra mai fù' are often known as 'Handel's Largo', even though the original tempo marking was 'Larghetto' (meaning a little less 'broad' than usually understood for plain Largo).

Opera in France

An independent French tradition of opera developed in the late 17th century. Opera was staged at the court of Louis XIV, under his patronage; so everything had to be grand, even spectacular, to glorify the king and the French nation. Ironically it was Lully – Italian by birth – who played the major role in establishing French opera. Earlier in his career he had composed *comédie-ballets* ('comedy ballets'), with spoken dialogue as well as dancing, singing and instrumental music, including *Le Bourgeois gentilhomme* ('The middle-class nobleman', 1670).

His opera *Cadmus et Hermione* dates from 1673. Like many French Baroque operas, it was termed a *tragédie en musique* ('tragedy in music'), although, typically for this genre, there was a happy not a tragic ending. The story of Cadmus and Hermione was from classical mythology, as usual for Lully's operas. In the prelude, Louis XIV is glorified by being depicted as the god Apollo killing the Python of Delphi, a giant snake.

Rameau was the major French composer for the stage in the early 18th century. He composed several *tragédies en musique,* including *Dardanus* (1739). His *opéras-ballets* were shorter than *tragédies*, with three or four acts rather than five, each having a more or less separate plot. *Les Indes galantes* ('The Amorous Indies', 1735) is typical of *opéra-ballet* in its 'exotic' non-European settings, including the Peruvian mountains and a Persian market. ('The Indies', as in Rameau's title, could simply mean anywhere exotic, in effect 'not Europe'.)

Awareness of how different foreign societies were from European ones encouraged commentators like the French philosopher Jean-Jacques Rousseau (1712–1778) to argue that European culture corrupted people, while those in other cultures, though 'savage', were nevertheless 'noble'.

French operas tended to have more dancing than Italian operas, and more ensembles and choruses. Short 'airs' were preferred to extended arias. Recitative tended to be more melodious, less 'basic' than Italian *secco* recitative. Overtures were generally of the French type.

Stylised Chinese costume from Rameau's *Les Indes galantes*

French and Italian overtures

Baroque operas (except some of the earliest) opened with introductory instrumental music, known today as an overture. In Baroque operas the overture was rarely connected with the following action, whereas in later times it sometimes 'set the scene', perhaps by including themes from the opera itself, as in Weber's *Der Freischütz* ('The Marksman', 1821). There were two main types of overture – French and Italian.

A French overture – or *ouverture* (French for 'opening') – has a slow section and a quick section. The French overture pattern may be traceable to some early Italian opera overtures, such as Cavalli's in *Giasone* ('Jason', 1649), where a slow section is followed by a quick section (don't confuse this early Italian type with the later three-section Italian overture described below). There may then be a slow ending or even another slow section (perhaps based on the first), making the pattern S–Q–(S):

- S: the opening slow section sounds grand and full of pomp (as befitted French court opera), often with many dotted rhythms. It's in duple time, usually homophonic in texture, and is played twice.
- Q: the following quick section (sometimes dance-like) is usually in triple or compound time and fugal style, so that the main sections are usually contrasted in texture as well as in tempo.

Lully's first French overture belongs to his ballet *Alcidiane* (1658). French overtures were later used outside France, for example by Purcell in *Dido and Aeneas* (from the 1680s). They were not restricted to opera – for example, Handel's oratorio *Messiah* starts with one.

The French overture and some dances from an opera or ballet may sometimes have been performed together to make an orchestral suite. German composers adapted this idea. For example, Bach's four orchestral suites were originally called overtures – each having a specially composed French overture that was never part of an opera, plus 'modern' dances of the kinds favoured in French operas. Bach's Suite No. 3 in D has a French overture, the famous Air (see Chapter 2), Gavottes I and II, Bourrée, and Gigue. Bach's Keyboard Partita No. 4 also has a French overture, but is based on the traditional allemande–courante–sarabande–gigue pattern.

The Italian type of overture was quite different from the French. Developed by Alessandro Scarlatti, it was entitled '*Sinfonia*' or '*Sinfonia avanti l'opera*' – 'Symphony before the opera'. The earliest may be in Scarlatti's *La caduta de' Decemviri* (1697) – 'The Fall of the Decemviri'. (The *Decemviri*, literally 'the ten men', were a group of tyrants in ancient Rome, overthrown in 449BC.) An Italian overture had three sections, Q–S–Q. As time went on, sinfonias came to be performed on their own, and then were specially composed. Such sinfonias are among the ancestors of the symphonies of Haydn and Mozart with their three (or four) movements. Use of a minuet in many symphonies shows that orchestral suites were among other symphonic ancestors.

17. ORATORIOS AND PASSIONS

In Chapters 17 and 18 we consider chiefly music with religious words – 'sacred' music, as it is sometimes called. Some sacred music is 'church music' in the sense that it was designed for performance in services (this includes Bach's church cantatas). However, some religious works were not intended for such use – Handel's oratorios in particular were often performed in the theatre.

In Chapter 17 we deal first with oratorios, and then with another large-scale genre that had some links with it – the Passion. Chapter 18 begins with the cantata, a smaller-scale type of work. We look in that chapter also at two important works that stand out as major achievements in other genres – Bach's B minor Mass and Monteverdi's *Vespers*.

Oratorios

Oratorios are works with religious words, for soloist(s), choir and orchestra, in several movements. They were performed in church (but not within a service) or in a theatre. They were often similar in musical style and structure to operas, but generally there was no acting or scenery. Later ones are on a very large scale: Handel's *Messiah* (1741) – perhaps the most widely known of all oratorios – has about two and a half hours' worth of music. There's a section on this later in the chapter.

Italian origin and early history

In mid-16th-century Rome the name 'oratorio' was used, not for a piece of music, but for a special place for prayer connected with a religious order established by Filippo Neri (now often known as St Philip Neri, 1515–1595).* Religious meetings rather than formal religious services were held there, and were widely attended, partly because people were drawn in by special kinds of devotional songs. These were often *laude spirituali* ('spiritual praises'), songs with greater popular appeal than the more formal church music of the time. They didn't have words from the Bible, as much church music did, and were in Italian not Latin, with the result that people understood better what they were singing about.

> *Compare this with the English word 'oratory', as in Brompton Oratory, a large Roman Catholic church in London.

Occasionally this religious music was on a more ambitious scale. In 1600 Emilio de' Cavalieri (c. 1550–1602) published his *Rappresentatione di Anima et di Corpo* ('Representation of Soul and of Body'; WEM 2: 1 has an excerpt). It was staged, with acting and dancing, and the whole text was sung, some of it in the new monody style. Some people consider it a kind of sacred opera (because it was performed on stage), while others classify it as an oratorio. It really belongs to a type of religious play which sometimes included music. But we can see it as a *forerunner* of oratorio.

By the mid-17th century the word 'oratorio' was applied to some of the musical works used in oratories. These were partly descendants of the 'spiritual madrigals' which Giovanni Francesco Anerio (c. 1567–1630) published in Rome in 1619 with the title *Teatro armonico spirituale di madrigali* (literally 'The harmonious spiritual theatre of madrigals'). These works, despite the title, were not acted. They were settings of stories from the Bible or about the saints, with different singers for different characters, and with a chorus which sometimes acted as narrator.

Giacomo Carissimi (1605–1674) was the first important composer of oratorios. His works include *Jephte* (written before 1648) and *Jonas* (date uncertain). *Jephte* is based on the story of Jephthah from the Bible (see Judges 10–12, especially 11: 29–40). *Jonas* deals with the story of Jonah from the Bible, in which the prophet was swallowed (but later regurgitated) by a large sea creature after being shipwrecked. Carissimi makes the most of the dramatic episodes from both stories, with, for example, a battle scene in *Jephte* and a storm at sea in *Jonas*. Both works have Latin words, based on rather than directly quoting from the Bible at length, and were performed at the Crocifisso (Italian: 'Crucifix') oratory in Rome, which was attended by many noblemen from the city.

Carissimi's oratorios were not yet on the grand Handelian scale (*Jephte* lasts about 25 minutes). But they were known to Handel, who appears to have used one of Carissimi's choruses as the basis for a movement in the oratorio *Samson* (1743). Interestingly, one of Handel's last oratorios, composed in 1751, and entitled *Jephtha*, shared its central character with Carissimi's *Jephte*.

By the late 17th century oratorios were composed in various Italian cities, and in other countries – for example it was soon accepted at the (Catholic) emperor's court in Vienna. In fact, the first oratorio performed there was by Emperor Leopold I himself (see Chapter 4, page 12) – *Il sacrifizio d'Abramo* ('The sacrifice of Abraham', 1660).

Oratorios were sometimes performed in the palaces of aristocrats as a form of semi-religious entertainment during Lent when theatres were closed and opera could not be staged. Lent is the six-week period before Easter in which Christians remember Jesus Christ's fasting in the wilderness, and his Passion (sufferings and death). Traditionally people led a plainer, stricter life in Lent, and many church leaders in the Baroque period mistrusted all theatre (including opera) as immoral or frivolous. But Alessandro Scarlatti's *Cain, or the First Murder* (in Italian: *Cain, ovvero il primo omicidio*), performed in Venice in 1707 and Rome in 1710, no doubt had some of the appeal of a thriller, as well as a more serious religious purpose. (The original story is from Genesis, chapter 4.)

Handel's oratorios

At almost the same time, Handel, then a young man resident in Rome, composed *Oratorio per la Resurrezione* (Italian: 'Oratorio for the Resurrection', 1708). Early 18th-century Italian oratorios, such as this and Alessandro Scarlatti's *Cain*, were sometimes allowed as a substitute for opera – especially in Rome where in 1701 Pope Clement XI had banned public performances of opera (even outside Lent).

In London too, where Handel took up residence a few years later, composers needed to tread warily. In 1732 he planned a staged performance of *Esther*, an oratorio composed in 1718 for the duke of Chandos. This was to be in a theatre, but the bishop of London objected to the staging of a piece on a biblical subject. Handel compromised by giving the work in a concert version (although still in the theatre).

This was very successful, and shortly afterwards he composed *Deborah* and *Athalia*, which, like his later oratorios as well, were designed for unstaged performance, despite the strong dramatic element (which came naturally to him as a major opera composer). Handel, although not a native of England, knew its people well enough to realise that they would find 'music joined to poetry … not an entertainment for an evening, and that something that had the appearance of a plot or fable was necessary to keep their attention awake' (Sir John Hawkins (1719–1789), writer of an early history of music).

With *Esther*, *Deborah* and *Athalia* Handel established the oratorio in England, continuing with a series of major works through to the early 1750s. He followed Italian rather than German practice by basing his works on Old Testament stories rather than by directly setting extended passages from the Bible.

Messiah

Messiah was composed in about three weeks in 1741, and first performed in Dublin, Ireland (then part of the United Kingdom). Unlike most of Handel's oratorios, its text is directly from the Bible, rather than *based* on it – to get round possible objections to singing biblical words in the theatre, Handel used to perform *Messiah* for charity. The 'Messiah' is Jesus Christ, but there's nothing about his life apart from a few verses from the Christmas story. The text is a collection of Old Testament prophecies, with a few New Testament passages that explain the significance of Christ's resurrection. *Messiah*, as usual for Handel's oratorios, has three parts.

Choruses are plentiful, whereas in operas they are very few. This is partly why *Messiah* has been so popular with British choral societies, and why *Israel in Egypt* (1738), with its even greater emphasis on choruses, was once so widely sung. The choruses show great variety – compare, for example, the intense minor-key anguish of 'And with his stripes [injuries or beatings] we are healed' (a fugue) and the exciting major-key triumph of the well-known 'Hallelujah' chorus (mostly homophonic).* There may be considerable variety within a chorus, sometimes to allow word-painting; for example, in 'Glory to God in the highest' the opening is for high voices, with a vigorous orchestral part, whereas 'and peace on earth' is both lower and slower.

---

*There's a tradition that King George II was so moved when he heard the 'Hallelujah' chorus that he stood up. Other people weren't allowed to sit while the king stood, so it became (as it still is) the custom for audiences to rise for this chorus.

A performance of *Messiah* at the BBC Proms in the Royal Albert Hall, London

The first chorus in *Messiah* is 'And the glory of the Lord'. Following on from the first recitative and the first aria, it completes a section with text from the poem of encouragement and consolation in Isaiah, chapter 40. Appropriately, an optimistic mood prevails throughout the chorus, with everything in a major key. The text has four phrases: (a) 'And the glory, the glory of the Lord',* (b) 'shall be revealed', (c) 'and all flesh [humankind] shall see it together' and (d) 'for the mouth of the Lord hath spoken it.'

*Repetition of 'the glory' in the first phrase may be for emphasis – or to make the words fit an existing melody, specifically one from Rameau's *Les Fêtes d'Hébé* (1739). For more on Handel's borrowing from other composers, see Chapter 20.

Handel generally associated one melodic idea with each phrase of text, but ideas are often combined, with great resourcefulness and lightness of touch. In the instrumental introduction we hear ideas (a) and (b) successively, in violin 1. Altos and tenors take up these ideas, which are then combined in full four-part writing. After a short interlude based on (b), idea (c) is sung by altos, then tenors, before tenors and basses together introduce a weightier theme, (d). Having exposed all four themes, Handel rings the changes for the rest of the chorus, clearly enjoying the feat of working (a), (c) and (d) together near the end.

There are many beautiful arias in *Messiah*, including 'He shall feed his flock' from Act 1 and 'I know that my Redeemer liveth' from Part 3 – Handel had a superb gift for melody. 'He was despised and rejected' from Part 2 conveys wonderfully the rejected Messiah's grief, yet perhaps surprisingly much of it is in a major key. The music is much broken by rests, to symbolise Christ's desolation – in the music example below the singer is at times completely unsupported. The sustained chord is a diminished 7th, one which Baroque composers tended to reserve for moments of special intensity.

Handel, 'He was despised' from *Messiah*, Part 2

The bass aria 'Why do the nations', full of violent energy, is a complete contrast. The orchestra begins with pounding quaver Cs in the bass under rapid repeated-note and rising arpeggio shapes. The beginning of the introduction is then heard again as the soloist enters with the melody in the example below – storming up a broken chord of C major before rushing headlong down the scale. For Christians, the text from the Old Testament Psalm 2 refers to the actions of the enemies of Christ and his church, a theme taken up again in the following chorus 'Let us break'. God's vengeance is taken in the next aria ('Thou shalt break them'), and victory is celebrated in the 'Hallelujah' chorus.

Handel, 'Why do the nations', from *Messiah*, Part 2

Germany: Historia, Passion and Oratorio

In the 17th century Protestant areas of Germany had their own genre, the *historia* (Latin: 'story', not 'history' – plural *historiae*), in which a section of the Bible was set to music, especially the story of Christ's Passion. As we've seen, Italian oratorios didn't as a rule quote at length from the Bible, but were *based* on biblical stories.

Heinrich Schütz composed several very important *historiae*, including the 'Christmas Story' (published 1664). The original German title is sometimes shortened to *Historia der Geburt Jesu Christi* ('The story of the birth of Jesus Christ'). The words are from the Gospels of St Matthew and St Luke in the Bible. The narrator's part (labelled 'Evangelist', that is, the Gospel writer), for tenor, is recitative with basso continuo. This alternates with pieces for the Angel, the Shepherds, the Magi (Wise Men) and others, for various combinations of solo and choral voices and instruments. Herod, for example, is a bass with (appropriately for a king) two trumpets and continuo. His opening command to the Magi to find the baby Jesus, with its rising melismas over a sustained low note, brilliantly combines the grandeur of a king with the menace of a tyrant:

Schütz, 'Ziehet hin' from *Historia der Geburt Jesu Christi* (the 'Christmas Story')

Some German composers introduced some non-biblical words into Passion *historiae*, and these 'hybrid' works are sometimes called 'oratorio Passions'. J. S. Bach's *St Matthew Passion* (in German, *Matthäus-Passion*, 1727) is a late example, and one of the finest works of the late Baroque: we will look at it a little more closely below. Bach's musically rich and varied setting of the Passion is very different from Schütz's austere *historia* of the same name (1666). The latter has just recitatives and a few brief ensembles, and all singing is unaccompanied, probably because of an ancient custom that instruments remained silent in Holy Week (the week before Easter).

*As well as 'oratorio Passions' there were 'Passion oratorios', which tell the Passion story in verse rather than by using the actual biblical words.

By the early 18th century the word 'oratorio' was sometimes used quite loosely in Germany – for example, Bach's 'Christmas Oratorio' (*Weihnachts-Oratorium*) is really a set of six cantatas first performed on six different days between Christmas 1734 and Epiphany (6 January) 1735.

Bach's St Matthew Passion

Bach used recitative to set the biblical words, from St Matthew's Gospel, chapters 26 and 27, in German. These words are chiefly narrative, sung by the Evangelist (a tenor). The words of Jesus and other individuals, including Peter, Judas, and Pilate, are taken by other soloists (Jesus by a bass, for example). The Evangelist's part is in the *secco* recitative tradition, as can be heard clearly from his opening announcement ('Da Jesus diese Rede vollendet hatte' = 'When Jesus had finished all these sayings').

The part of Jesus is given special solemnity: even when his recitative is in the *secco* style, the accompaniment is fully notated for strings, not just improvised on the organ. There are moments where the harmony is of great chromatic intensity, or the melodic line almost literally tortured, as when Jesus predicts at the end of the first recitative that he will be crucified ('gekreuziget'):

Bach, first recitative from *St Matthew Passion*

The words of the crowd are for choir, with short accompanied outbursts (notably where they yell out 'Barabbas' to a violent diminished 7th chord) and slightly more extended contrapuntal passages (for example where they demand Jesus' crucifixion).

The arias draw on verse by C.F. Henrici, who is usually known by his pen-name Picander. So actually do some of the elaborate *accompagnato* (i.e. non-*secco*) recitatives, including 'Du lieber Heiland' ('Thou beloved Saviour') from Part 1 and 'Ach Golgatha, unselges Golgatha' ('Ah Golgotha, unhappy Golgotha')* from Part 2. Arias and accompanied recitatives are used to comment on the narrative, with the aim of encouraging listeners' religious devotion. For example in 'Gerne will ich mich bequemen' ('Gladly would I submit') the singer expresses willingness to share in Christ's sufferings.

*Golgotha (otherwise known as Calvary) is the place where Jesus was crucified.

The alto aria 'Erbarme dich, mein Gott' ('Have mercy, my God') is exceptionally moving, not least because of its intensely expressive obbligato violin part, some of the descending patterns probably representing falling tears. 'Erbarme dich' is sung just after Jesus' leading disciple Peter has denied knowledge of his master three times. Peter is overcome with grief and remorse (the Bible says that he wept bitterly) but Bach's aria, although far from bright and cheerful, is not negative or depressing, despite never cadencing in a major key in six or seven minutes. After all, the composer and his 18th-century listeners knew that Peter's repeated cries for mercy and forgiveness were granted abundantly by Jesus after his resurrection.

Many choruses in the *St Matthew Passion* are single-verse four-part harmonisations of chorales in homophonic style, with orchestra doubling the vocal parts.* The traditional words and melodies were familiar to Bach's listeners, and no doubt came as a relief to those who were not admirers of his more complex and learned music. We hear five times a melody now often known as the 'Passion chorale'. The last harmonisation, which follows Jesus' death on the cross, is particularly intense, with some remarkable chromatic harmony. Instead of ending in a major key as in the other four versions, Bach finally acknowledges that the 'Passion chorale' melody was originally a minor phrygian-mode tune, and ends with an unusual modal-style cadence.

*You may be familiar with four-part chorale harmonisations from working on 'Bach chorales' in music exams. Most of the pieces you will have studied come from Bach's cantatas and Passions, and are available in a collection called *Bach Riemenschneider – 371 Harmonized Chorales* (Schirmer, 1941).

Some choruses have texts by Picander, including the final great C minor 'Wir setzen uns mit Tränen nieder' ('We lay ourselves down with tears', DMBE 2: 9). Here, as in a number of other non-chorale choruses, there are two four-part choirs, who sometimes share the same material, sometimes alternate in antiphony. The opening movement ('Kommt, ihr Töchter, helft mir klagen' = 'Come, you daughters, help me lament') has even more striking use of choral resources: a special soprano section sings a chorale against a setting of words by Picander for the two four-part choirs. The second four-part choir shouts out a series of one-word questions (in English = 'whom?' 'how?', 'what?', 'where?'), interrupting the first choir, who urge us to see the 'bridegroom ... like a lamb ... in patience ... looking on our faults.'

18. CANTATAS, AND TWO OTHER MAJOR WORKS

Cantatas

Cantata is Italian for 'sung'. In the early 17th century the word was sometimes used for more or less any sung piece, but came to mean a work for voice(s) and instruments in several movements. A cantata was generally shorter than an oratorio, sometimes without chorus, and could be sacred or secular.

Late Baroque Italian cantatas

Cantatas were widely composed in Italy in the late Baroque period – most were secular and generally about love. Alessandro Scarlatti composed roughly 600. Most are for a single voice (commonly soprano) but some are duets. There is often just a continuo accompaniment.

Alessandro Scarlatti, part of the first recitative from *Mitilde, mio tesor*

Scarlatti's cantatas frequently have two or three recitative-aria pairs – rather like an (unstaged) mini-opera with two or three scenes. A fine example is *Mitilde, mio tesor* ('Matilda, my treasure'), a cantata named after the recitative with which the work begins. This first recitative (see the music example opposite) has a remarkable modulation to illustrate the words 'nel duol d'aspri tormenti' ('in the sorrow of bitter torments'). Such writing didn't please everyone: one critic described Scarlatti's harmony generally as 'extravagant and irregular'.

Nowadays Scarlatti's Christmas cantata *Oh di Betlemme altera povertà venturosa* ('O noble and fortunate poverty of Bethlehem') is his best known; DMBE 1: 12 has one of the arias, for soprano, strings and continuo. Despite the religious words, it was not for church services (where Latin, not Italian, was used) but possibly for a Christmas meeting of the Arcadian Academy – a group of musicians, poets and philosophers founded in Rome in 1690.

Handel composed some of his many Italian secular cantatas for the Arcadian Academy in the early 1700s. These sometimes follow closely the cantata pattern established by Scarlatti.

J. S. Bach's cantatas

The secular cantata was much less important in Germany, where the majority of cantatas were for the church. Bach did however compose a considerable number, of which about 30 survive, for special occasions including royal birthdays. The 'Coffee' cantata (BWV 211), for the Leipzig *Collegium Musicum*, was performed in a coffee house.

Bach's church cantatas, like Italian secular ones, include recitatives and arias, but most have choruses as well. It may seem odd that *church* works had recitatives and arias, which had originated in opera, a *secular* genre. But at the end of the 17th century, some German writers tried to modernise church music by providing composers with texts that included specially written religious poetry.* Erdmann Neumeister (1671–1756) drew a comparison with opera, and used the term 'cantata'. Usually at that time a church cantata was known as a concerto, or simply as a *Kirchenstück* ('church piece') or *Kirchenmusik*. Johann Philipp Krieger (1649–1725) and Johann Kuhnau (1660–1722), Bach's predecessor at St Thomas's church, Leipzig, were among the earliest composers of the newer cantata.

*Previously church music in Germany had tended to concentrate on passages from the Bible and on chorales.

Statue of Bach outside St Thomas's church, Leipzig

Although not published in his lifetime, the church cantatas are central to Bach's work. About 200 survive, but there appear originally to have been more than 300, with five main sets, each covering every Sunday and major holy day of the church's year. Early 18th-century German composers often wrote such yearly cycles of cantatas – Telemann produced more than 20.

Bach's cantatas were mostly composed for performance during Sunday morning services at Leipzig, after the Gospel (a reading from one of the New Testament gospels – Matthew, Mark, Luke or John), so as to underline its theme, and before the Creed (a statement of Christian belief) and the sermon. However, some cantatas, including Cantata No. 147, were divided into two, the second part following the sermon. As you can imagine, Bach's Sunday morning service was lengthy – the cantata alone might last for 20 minutes or more.

Cantata No. 147, *Herz und Mund und Tat und Leben*, ('Heart and mouth and deed and life'), was designed for the feast of the Visitation of the Virgin Mary (see St Luke's Gospel 1: 36–45). Completed in 1723, it was a revision of a cantata composed in about 1716 for a different feast. The well-known piece 'Jesu, joy of man's desiring' (see musical example below) comes from this cantata.

J. S. Bach, part of the chorus 'Wohl mir, dass ich Jesum habe' ('Jesu, joy of man's desiring'), the sixth movement of Cantata No. 147 (BWV 147), *Herz und Mund und Tat und Leben*

The introduction continues for six more bars, then the voices enter:

Like many cantatas, No. 147:

- Begins with a chorus
- Has solo recitatives and arias
- Ends with a chorus, based on a chorale.

Here's the scheme in detail. Four soloists are required (soprano, alto, tenor, bass):

Part I
1. Chorus – lively, featuring a solo trumpet
2. Recitative *stromentato* – tenor
3. Aria – alto, with oboe d'amore obbligato and continuo
4. Recitative *secco* – bass
5. Aria – soprano, with violin obbligato and continuo
6. Chorus – 'Wohl mir, dass ich Jesum habe' ('[It's] well for me that I have Jesus') = 'Jesu, joy' for the first time – four-part choir (sopranos singing the chorale), plus strings and oboes. A trumpet doubles the chorale melody.

The oboe d'amore, which Bach required in No. 3, was pitched a minor 3rd lower than the ordinary oboe and had a quieter sound (which would combine well with the alto soloist). Despite the Italian name (literally meaning 'oboe of love') this instrument was of early 18th-century German origin. (In fact, Bach's own city of Leipzig was an important centre of oboe d'amore production.) The instrument was widely used, though only briefly, but it was revived in a small way in the 19th century and there is a part for it in Ravel's *Boléro*. The word 'obbligato' (as in Nos. 3 and 5) refers to an obligatory (that is, essential) solo instrument. In each case this provides an additional independent melodic part, in addition to the vocal part and continuo.

Part 2
7. Aria – tenor and continuo
8. Recitative *stromentato* – alto, with oboe da caccia and continuo
9. Aria – bass, with trumpet obbligato, strings (doubled by oboes) and continuo
10. Chorus – 'Jesus bleibet meine Freude' ('Jesus remains my joy') – same music as No. 6.

Note that an aria such as No. 7 with voice and continuo only – and therefore without obbligato instrument(s) – is often called a 'continuo aria'. The oboe da caccia, as required in No. 8, was pitched a 5th lower than the ordinary oboe, and was therefore similar in range to the present-day cor anglais. Despite its name, which meant 'oboe of the hunt', the sound was gentle and expressive, combining well with the alto solo voice here, as the oboe d'amore does in No. 3.

Nos. 6 and 10 are quite elaborate treatments of a chorale melody, with instrumental passages at the beginning and after each phrase of the chorale.

It was common for cantatas to end with a more straightforward treatment of a chorale in which the kind of homophonic vocal writing for choir and congregation found in Nos. 6 and 10 of Cantata No. 147 was merely doubled by the orchestra. An example is the final movement of Cantata No. 80, *Ein' feste Burg* ('[Our God is] a sure stronghold').

Bach's B minor Mass

In Chapters 13–18 so far we have described genres and then have referred to examples. A different approach is to focus on a major work straight away, and then try to understand something of its background – which is what often happens in our real-life listening experience.

J.S. Bach's B minor Mass, one of the outstanding achievements of Baroque music, has a remarkable history. Bach wrote parts of it in the 1720s and 30s, but returned to it in the late 1740s, aiming, it seems, to provide a grand demonstration of his skills in sacred music rather than a work for regular performance. Often he adapted earlier pieces, presumably ones that he regarded particularly highly. For example, the choral fugue at 'Gratias agimus' ('We give thanks') is very closely modelled on a movement with German words that mean the same ('Wir danken dir') from Cantata No. 29. The 'Gratias agimus' fugue is repeated at the end of the mass ('Dona nobis pacem' = 'Grant us peace') with small rhythmic changes designed to accommodate the different words.

Bach took his texts from the Mass, the principal Roman Catholic act of worship (which corresponds in some ways to the communion or eucharistic services of other Christian churches). The words are in Latin, apart from those of the Kyrie, which, following a very ancient tradition, are in Greek. Bach divides the B minor Mass into four main parts, each split into shorter movements, some for solo voices, others for four- or five-part choir.

Bach's four principal parts begin:

- Kyrie eleison ('Lord, have mercy')
- Gloria in excelsis Deo ('Glory in the heights to God')
- Credo ('I believe [in one God]')
- Sanctus ('Holy, [holy, holy]')

> This includes a section usually regarded as separate from the Sanctus, namely the Agnus Dei ('Lamb of God').

In 1733 Bach completed the Kyrie and Gloria, which are on a vast scale (together they last about an hour), and presented them to the new elector* of Saxony, Friedrich August II. As Bach was a Lutheran, you might not expect him to provide a work for a Roman Catholic elector, but he wanted a favour – the title of court composer – something which was granted in 1736. And in any case 'short' masses with just Kyrie and Gloria were also sometimes performed in Lutheran churches.

> *Electors were princes or archbishops in the Holy Roman Empire who together elected the emperor.

The 1733 work was probably performed in a service shortly after composition, despite its length. The mass as a whole, complete with Credo and Sanctus, was far too extended (at about two hours) to be performed in that way, and was apparently never heard in full until the mid-19th century, when it was performed in a concert setting. Bach was much inclined in the late 1740s to write more for his own satisfaction than with performance directly in mind (see Chapter 19, end of section 'Bach at work').

The Credo demonstrates the work's variety of style and texture particularly well. The opening chorus, 'Credo in unum Deum' ('I believe in one God') is a fugue whose subject is based on a plainsong phrase traditionally associated with these words. This subject is presented in long notes (mostly semibreves), starting with the tenors, the accompanying parts providing more varied rhythms. The rather severe style of counterpoint can be heard as a kind of partially modernised *stile antico* – with a largely independent orchestra part over a crotchet walking bass.

Bach, 'Credo' from B minor Mass

At the heart of the Credo text are the sections concerning Christ's incarnation (his being born as a human, while still remaining divine), and his crucifixion and death. The 'Et incarnatus', one of the last pieces that Bach composed, has an aching intensity largely due to the upward-resolving appoggiaturas heard on beats 2 and 3 of almost every bar. The pain of the cross is already in prospect even as Jesus is born.

For the 'Crucifixus' Bach borrowed part of a cantata movement composed right back in 1714. The handling of the descending chromatic ground bass is even more affecting than Purcell's in Dido's celebrated lament. One of the most wonderful moments in all music comes at the end – after so much minor-key music Bach unexpectedly ends in the relative major, G major. Christ is now buried (note how low the sopranos are in particular), his sufferings over, and the resurrection assured.

The 'Crucifixus' from Bach's autograph score of the B minor Mass

There can be no mistaking Christ's rising again ('Et resurrexit'), with the brilliant D major trumpet writing and joyful melismatic passages for choir.

Bach, 'Et resurrexit' from B minor Mass

Monteverdi's Vespers (1610)

The work usually referred to as 'Monteverdi's Vespers' was published in Venice in 1610, but on the title-page 'Vesperae' (Latin for the afternoon or evening service of 'Vespers') is printed so small that you could easily miss it.

Title page from Monteverdi's *Vespers*

The words that really stand out are 'Sanctissimae Virgini missa senis vocibus' (Latin: 'To the most holy Virgin [Mary], mass for six voices). This six-part mass is for voices only, in the *stile antico*, showing reverence for tradition ahead of the *stile moderno* of the Vespers. Monteverdi, after all, was dedicating the volume to Pope Paul V, a rather uncompromising figure who was always intent on upholding the authority and privileges of the Church. Monteverdi may have hoped (in vain as it turned out) to secure a musical appointment in Rome. His appeal to tradition extends to use of 'parody',* for he reworked ideas from the motet *In illo tempore* by Nicolas Gombert (c. 1495–c. 1560). Although Gombert's motet had probably been composed no more than about 60 or 70 years previously, this was pretty old by early 17th-century standards (see Chapter 3, page 10).

*A technique used especially in the 16th century: a composer adapted and built on material from a previous work to demonstrate compositional skill and admiration for the original. It is quite different from the kind of parody where you produce a version of something to make fun of it, affectionately or otherwise (e.g. 'While shepherds washed their socks by night').

After the mass, there is music in more modern styles for Vespers, not all of which is likely to have been used on any one occasion. The opening versicle and response, 'Deus in adjutorium' ('O God, [hurry] to [my] aid', DMBE 1: 7), is one of the most striking pieces of church music ever, with its static vocal harmonies and fanfare-like accompaniment – it was adapted from the introductory instrumental toccata from the opera *Orfeo*. Monteverdi then provides settings of several psalms for large forces, with some sections based on plainsong melodies traditionally used for psalms. There are four 'concertos' for smaller forces, which could be used outside Vespers. (See chapter 8, section 'Venice: contrasts'.)

Monteverdi provided also a prayer to the Virgin Mary entitled 'Sonata: Sancta Maria, ora pro nobis' ('Holy Mary, pray for us'). In this a simple melody of narrow range is sung eleven times in slightly different versions, separated by long rests amidst a varied and lively instrumental accompaniment (the latter presumably justifying the title 'sonata' – usually reserved for instrumental music).

There follows a lovely setting of a hymn to the Virgin Mary, 'Ave maris stella' ('Hail, star of the sea'). In the music example below, Monteverdi has added one or two notes to the Dorian-mode plainsong (those with asterisks) to provide added melodic interest. Rhythmically his melody has pronounced contrasts between long and short notes, whereas the original plainsong, when sung on its own, was for the most part more even and flowing.

Monteverdi, 'Ave maris stella' from *Vespers* (1610)

The service of Vespers always included the Magnificat, the song of the Virgin Mary from Luke's gospel, chapter 1; Monteverdi provided a choice of two settings.

19. BACH AND HANDEL: THEIR LIVES

Bach and Handel were both outstanding composers – the two musical giants of their time, if not of the whole Baroque era. There are similarities: the music of both shows plenty of standard late Baroque features – the continuo principle, the system of major and minor keys and functional harmony, and so on. And it's fascinating that they were both born in 1685 (within a month of each other) in Germany (less than 100 miles apart). Interestingly, they never met, although Bach twice attempted to make contact with Handel.

But it's the *contrasts* that best reveal each composer's character and achievements:

Bach	Handel
From family of musicians – a musical career almost inevitable	His father (who died in 1697) originally opposed Handel's study of music
Married twice; 20 children*	Never married; no children
Always worked in Germany	Worked in Germany and Italy, but mainly in England
Composed **first and foremost** for the church (notably cantatas, organ music)	Composed **first and foremost** for the theatre (operas, oratorios)
Fairly prosperous – steady salaried jobs (necessary to support family)	Wealthy – more freelance activity (no wife or children to support)

*Many died very young, and more than 30 years separated the births of the oldest and youngest. At times the family may have been big, but 20 children never sat round the same table for breakfast.

Bach at work

Bach worked mainly as a church musician – in his early 20s he said that his main aim was to organise church music well – but he spent some years as a court musician.

- 1703–1707: Arnstadt, then Mühlhausen, church organist.
- 1708–1717: Weimar, court organist to Duke of Weimar, and from 1714 also directed the court orchestra, probably from the violin (his title was *Konzertmeister*, a word now used in Germany for the leading first violinist, 'leader of the orchestra').
- 1717–1723: Cöthen (now spelt Köthen). Musical director (*Kapellmeister*) to Prince Leopold of Anhalt-Cöthen.*
- 1723–1750: Leipzig, teacher at St Thomas's school and musical director at churches of St Thomas and St Nicholas. The school was attached to the main city church,

St Thomas's. Bach's official title was *Cantor*, literally 'singer' (modern spelling *Kantor*). He provided vocal and instrumental tuition, and was supposed to teach Latin (but in fact someone else did this).

■ He was also musical director at Leipzig University – from 1729 director of the *Collegium Musicum*, a music society which gave regular concerts.

Kapellmeister: literally 'chapel master'. *Kapelle* in German can mean any organised group of musicians (church or secular), whereas 'chapel' in English has only religious connections. The church attached to Prince Leopold's court had little music: it was Calvinist, and most Calvinists (unlike many Lutherans) regarded elaborate music in worship as distracting.

The high point in Bach's career was his time at Köthen. Prince Leopold was enthusiastic about music, and an ideal patron, until his marriage in 1721 to a wife with different interests. The work in Leipzig was important and more varied, but Bach had (socially at least) taken a step down, and he found working with the town and church authorities far from easy, particularly when he sensed that the status of music or his own rights were threatened. He was inclined to stubbornness and could be less than tactful.

Bach's various employments guided his choices as a composer. He composed much of his organ music at Weimar, for example. Some important instrumental music (including the *Brandenburg* concertos) dates from his time at Köthen. At Leipzig he composed many cantatas and other church music (including the *St Matthew Passion* and B minor Mass), and instrumental music.

Bach composed a good deal of keyboard music for pupils to play and as models for composition. Much was for advanced students, including his sons, such as the inventions and sinfonias (often known as the two-part and three-part inventions). But he did also compose straightforward pieces for his family, notably for his second wife Anna Magdalena.

Towards the end of his life Bach seems to have been writing increasingly for his own satisfaction (partly perhaps because difficulties with his Leipzig employers turned him in on himself). He sometimes became absorbed in elaborate and very learned contrapuntal writing – notably in *Die Kunst der Fuge* ('The Art of Fugue') for keyboard, written and revised at various times in the 1740s, and in the *Musikalisches Opfer* ('Musical Offering').

Bach was severely restricted in his last year or two by ill health and loss of sight, probably the result of diabetes (for which no effective treatment was then available).

Handel at work

Handel began largely as a composer of opera. Oratorio was a major interest in his later years:

■ 1703–1706: Hamburg, violinist and harpsichordist in opera company.
■ 1706–1710: Italy, composed for various aristocrats in Rome and Naples, visited Venice and Florence.

- 1710–1713: Hanover, director of music (Kapellmeister) to Elector of Hanover, but long periods in London.
- 1710–1740: London, composed operas, musical director of opera companies. From 1723 'composer of music for the Chapel Royal' and music master to royal princesses.
- 1732–1759: London, composed oratorios. He became increasingly self-employed, giving concerts of his own music. Gave concerts for charity – especially performances of *Messiah*.

Although Handel sometimes had financial worries, he made a great deal of money – for example, in 1737 he was paid £1,000 for two operas, more than £130,000 in terms of early 21st-century purchasing power. He was ambitious, and valued his independence. He enjoyed the patronage of aristocrats and royalty, but was more able than most musicians to be his own man, partly because from the early age of 28 he had a large annual pension from the British royal family. In recognition of his status, Handel was buried in Westminster Abbey.

GEORGE FREDERICK HANDEL Efq.ʳ
born February XXIII MDCLXXXIV.
died April XIV MDCCLIX. L.F.Roubiliac ino'et s

Handel's monument in Westminster Abbey

Whereas we now say that Handel was born in 1685, his date of birth is given on his monument in Westminster Abbey as 23 February 1684. In Handel's day, western European countries were slowly changing from the old Julian calendar (in which the year was reckoned to start on 25 March and end on 24 March) to the newer Gregorian calendar (which runs from 1 January to 31 December). So while we in the 21st century say that Handel was born in the second month of 1685, this older view places his date of birth late in 1684.

In financial and career terms Handel was far more successful than Bach. Generally speaking he got on better with other musicians and people in authority. However, one of the most widely known stories about him is of his quarrelling as a teenager with the composer Johann Mattheson. In the duel that followed, Handel had a lucky escape: one account says that a score which he carried in his coat deflected Mattheson's sword. Dr Charles Burney (1726–1814), one of the first English music historians, described Handel (later in life) as irritable at times, but essentially good-natured, possessing an 'original' sense of humour. His 'general look was somewhat heavy and sour; but when he *did* smile, it was [like] the sun, bursting out of a black cloud'.

Handel was not quite 20 when his first opera, *Almira, Königin von Castilien* ('Almira, Queen of Castile'), with German libretto, was staged at Hamburg in January 1705. While in Italy he wrote his first Italian operas, secular cantatas, and some church music with Latin words – for the Roman Catholic church although, like Bach, he was a Protestant. In London he was able to take advantage of a growing interest in Italian opera. He composed operas for the King's Theatre, Haymarket ('Queen's Theatre' in the reign of Queen Anne, who died in 1714) and for Covent Garden, working as musical director (1729–1734) for opera companies including the Royal Academy of Music (not to be confused with the modern-day music college of that name).

Difficulties with the politics and finance of the London opera world led Handel eventually to concentrate on oratorios. This suited him excellently. He could write recitatives and arias as in opera, and choruses (based partly on his experience of church music). He could also put on performances of concertos between acts, including his own organ concertos, with himself as the soloist.

Handel didn't compose much after the early 1750s – he had lost his sight by 1753. Incidentally, Handel and Bach were operated on by the same eye surgeon, in both cases with little success.

20. BACH AND HANDEL: THEIR MUSIC

Why were Bach and Handel such great composers?
The work of each is:

- Plentiful – there's lots of it
- Varied – with examples of different genres, performing forces, and a wide emotional range
- Excellent – in terms of ideas and how they are developed
- Different – it built on, rather than just repeated, what had been done by earlier composers
- Influential – many people over long periods of time have loved, respected and learned from it
- Challenging to the mind as well as powerful emotionally.

No other Baroque composers meet all these criteria quite so amply, however much we rightly admire Monteverdi, Schütz, Corelli, Vivaldi and others.

Contrasts

As we've seen, Bach composed first and foremost for the church, Handel for the theatre. Now some detail:

Bach	Handel
Church cantatas central to his output: German words	Operas central: Italian words
St Matthew and *St John Passions*: German words	Oratorios: English words (apart from the *Brockes Passion*, a Passion oratorio composed in the 1710s, with German words by B. H. Brockes)
Solo organ music for church	Organ concertos, as interval music for oratorio performances
Chorales much used in cantatas, passions and organ music	Chorales scarcely ever used
Many preludes and fugues for organ and keyboard	Less interest in fugue
Concertos blend Italian forms and styles (adopted from Vivaldi) with counterpoint in the north-German manner	Concertos could be played as interval music for oratorio performances, and their composition was not laboured over. Forms and style Italian-based (Corelli an important influence)

Some music for minor royal occasions and for civic ceremonies in Leipzig	Music for English coronation service of 1727 (including the anthem *Zadok the Priest*, also performed at every British coronation since 1727), and for other major royal and state occasions
Major church works include the B minor Mass and the Magnificat in D major, with Latin words, but for the German Lutheran church	Latin church music in his early days, for Roman Catholic churches in Italy
Music neglected in late 18th century, until 19th-century 'Bach revival' (see Chapter 21)	Reputation remained high after his death (although it rested mainly on a few oratorios and some instrumental music. His operas were long neglected: their true value has only recently been recognised)

For Bach the musical traditions of north Germany were central, but the influence of Italian instrumental music was strong. For Handel Italian influences were central. Both composers drew on French styles, notably in their suites and French overtures. In some of his vocal music Handel showed an awareness of English music, especially that of Purcell.

Bach's music is often elaborate, with plenty of counterpoint, and can be very intense, especially when a high level of dissonance helps to underline words expressing sorrow, grief or pain (as in parts of the *St Matthew Passion*, including the final chorus, DMBE 2: 19). Handel's music is usually less complex – more direct and immediately 'attractive'.

Contrasts: keyboard music

We could illustrate the contrasts between the two composers' approaches with reference to almost any genre. But a glance at their keyboard music may be particularly helpful.

Music for keyboard instruments – including both organ and harpsichord – was particularly important in the northern (Protestant) parts of Germany. As Bach always worked there, it's not surprising that his keyboard music is more significant than Handel's (which was composed mostly in Italy and England).

For the organ, Bach mainly wrote pieces based on chorales, preludes and fugues, and the six sonatas (see Chapter 14). Much of his organ music was written early in his career.

The 'Prelude' from the Prelude and Fugue in G major (BWV 550) appears as DMBE 2: 5. Sometimes Bach pairs a fugue with a fantasia or a toccata. Fantasias and toccatas tend to be more showy than preludes.

Handel wrote no music specifically for organ solo, but pioneered the organ concerto in his later years. His *Six Fugues or Voluntarys* (note the 18th-century spelling!) were however said to be for organ or harpsichord when published in the 1730s. (See Chapter 15 for more on Handel's concertos. His harpsichord music (mostly early) includes some suites which, although very fine, have received much less attention than the suites by Bach discussed in Chapter 13.)

The organ concertos, for the theatre, are mainly light and easy to listen to rather than intense and serious like most of Bach's organ music for church. In any case, English organs were smaller and gentler in sound than Bach's German instruments. Often there was just one manual, and usually no pedals – so that Handel's *Six Fugues* could easily be played on either harpsichord or organ.

Two works which highlight the differences between Handel's 'relaxed' approach and Bach's more systematic and learned methods are Handel's Organ Concerto Op. 7 No. 3 in B♭ and Bach's Prelude and *St Anne* Fugue in E♭.

Handel: Organ Concerto Op. 7 No. 3 in B♭

Because Handel himself played the solo parts in his organ concertos and directed the other players, he sometimes didn't bother to write everything out in full. Charles Burney noted that the parts he gave the band only contained the passages where they played themselves (Burney calls them the 'ritornels', an English version of the word 'ritornellos'). Handel improvised the solo part, and the success of the performance would have depended on his cuing the other players as to when to come in.

Sir John Hawkins tells us that Handel used to begin by improvising an introductory movement. The music:

'… stole on the ear in a slow and solemn progression; the harmony close wrought, and as full as could possibly be expressed … the whole … carrying the appearance of great simplicity. This kind of prelude was succeeded by the concerto itself, which he executed with a degree of spirit and firmness that no one ever pretended to equal.'

The first written-out movement in Op. 7 No. 3 (1751) begins by referring to the 'Hallelujah' chorus, which may imply that the concerto was sometimes used during performances of *Messiah*. Incidentally, Handel's earliest version of Op. 7 No. 3 didn't include these bars.

Handel, Concerto Op. 7 No. 3 in B♭ major, first movement

After this movement there's the choice of going straight on to a quick movement headed 'Spiritoso', or of inserting additional music for organ solo – though no music is actually given at this point. Handel's manuscript copy suggests that he would have improvised a slow movement and a fugue. Present-day organists usually prefer to borrow suitable movements from other music by Handel (for example from the *Six Fugues*).

The opening fugal theme of the 'Spiritoso' was taken from a mass by F. J. Habermann (1706–1783). Nowadays 'borrowing' from other composers *without acknowledging it* is termed plagiarism and is regarded as totally unacceptable (it is strictly forbidden in examinations, for example). Handel wasn't the only composer at the time to borrow from others, but he was apparently unique in the *amount* of such borrowing. His borrowing from others sometimes involved much more than using someone else's theme. For example, in the oratorio *Israel in Egypt* the chorus 'Egypt was glad' is a close adaptation of an instrumental canzona by Johann Caspar Kerll (1627–1693).

Handel's borrowings from others also reflected his admiration for the music concerned, which he is likely to have studied closely and learned from. He often borrowed from himself as well, as did Bach. Bach's known borrowings from others are relatively few, though. It appears that the second movement from the Harpsichord Concerto in F minor, BWV 1056 is indebted to a movement from a concerto by Telemann for oboe or flute and strings (TWV 51: G2). All types of borrowing helped to save time when new works were required at short notice.

For Bach's Harpsichord Concerto in F minor, 2nd movement, see DMBE 2: 10.

Bach: Prelude and *St Anne* Fugue in E♭

The Prelude and *St Anne* Fugue in E♭ (BWV 552) shows brilliantly the breadth of Bach's musical knowledge and experience, and his seriousness of purpose. The fugue is so named because its subject opens with a strong (but chance) resemblance to the hymn tune 'St Anne' ('O God, our help in ages past'). More significant is the brief similarity to the fugue subject in the second section of Buxtehude's Prelude in E (BuxWV 141): Bach regarded Buxtehude's music very highly, even travelling 200 miles on foot as a young man to hear the master play.

The Prelude and Fugue were probably intended to be played together, despite standing at opposite ends of the book in which they were published – Part 3 of Bach's *Clavierübung* (published at Leipzig in 1739). This volume contained mostly chorale-based pieces and was dedicated to 'lovers of music, and especially for connoisseurs' (that is, experts and good judges of the subject).

Clavierübung literally means 'keyboard practice'. However, practice doesn't mean material for practising (exercises and the like). Bach is practising the art of music, rather as a doctor practises medicine. Only Part 3 of *Clavierübung* is for organ – the other three parts are for harpsichord.

The Prelude and Fugue show Bach's characteristic skill in bringing together styles from different countries. The Prelude begins like a French overture, with its grand-sounding dotted rhythms. But in terms of structure it is based on the concerto, a genre of Italian origin. The magnificent 'French overture' ritornello with pedals alternates with quieter 'solo' passages (often without pedals). The Fugue shows Bach's grounding in the German contrapuntal tradition.

The Prelude and Fugue demonstrate Bach's love of number symbolism. They have numerous references to '3', perhaps to match the number of the Holy Trinity (Father, Son and Holy Spirit) – hence the fugue's other nickname, the 'Trinity' fugue. Note, for example, the three flats of the key signature and the three sections of the fugue. Other threes in the fugue concern numbers of bars: sections 1 and 3 have 36 bars each (3 x 12); section 2 has 45 bars (3 x 15). Despite all this, the music doesn't sound dry and mathematical. There are many examples of number symbolism elsewhere in Bach. For instance, the organ fughetta (short fugue) 'Dies sind die heil'gen zehn Gebot' ('These are the holy ten commandments'), BWV 679, has ten entries of the fugal subject. Bach was deeply fascinated by the number 14, the sum of the letters of his name (B = 2, A = 1, C = 3, H = 8, total = 14), and waited eight years before joining a learned musical society in Leipzig as the 14th member!

As well as using number symbolism, Bach sometimes made music out of his name. In the last (14th) fugue from *Die Kunst der Fuge* ('The Art of Fugue') the four-note pattern B♭–A–C–B♮ spells B-A-C-H if you use the German system of letter names, where B = our B♭ and H = B♮.

Usually Bach's fugues run straight through, without clear breaks. However, in the *St Anne* fugue he seems to be looking back to the 17th century when fugues were sometimes in separate sections.

Contrasts: special projects for Handel and Bach

In 1749 Handel was asked to compose special music for the festivities, complete with fireworks, planned by the British royal family and government in celebration of the Treaty of Aix-la-Chapelle (1748). This treaty, signed by leading European monarchs, concluded the War of the Austrian Succession. Among many other things it confirmed the right of George II and his successors to the British throne.

Handel's response to his commission was to create a suite, the *Music for the Royal Fireworks*. Even the dress rehearsal attracted thousands of people, and the music has been popular ever since. With its simple harmonic language, and fine dignified tunes, Handel was able to capture perfectly, and to build on, the national mood of rejoicing – despite the fact that the longest movement was a *French* overture, and two other movements have French titles: 'La Paix' ('Peace') and 'La Réjouissance' ('Rejoicing'). Remember though that George II claimed (for historical reasons that need not concern us here) to be king of France as well as of Great Britain and Ireland.

Two years earlier Bach had been asked to visit the court of King Frederick the Great of Prussia (flautist, composer, and an enthusiastic patron of music), where his second son Carl Philipp Emanuel (1714–1788) worked as a musician. Bach senior improvised at the piano on a theme given to him by the king.* After returning home to Leipzig he worked on the theme further, producing a series of movements, some of them complicated canons (in one of these, one part plays an extended version of the royal theme while the other plays the same material *backwards*, to make a canon *cancrizans* – 'crab canon'). Everything was published and dedicated to the king as the *Musikalisches Opfer* ('Musical Offering'), but the style and content were both too learned for his liking – no lasting benefit came to Bach.

*It's worth remembering that pianos were still a novelty at this time, even though the first examples, made by Cristofori in Italy, date back to c. 1700. King Frederick's pianos were made by Silbermann, and J. S. Bach is said to have been impressed. The action was simpler and lighter, and the sound thinner and smaller than on a modern piano.

Frederick the Great playing the flute with Bach at the harpsichord

You might say that Bach made a misjudgement that Handel would never have made. But the real point of these two stories is – once again – that two extremely important composers were very different men with vastly different priorities.

21. THE END OF THE BAROQUE PERIOD – AND BEYOND

From Baroque to Classical

The Baroque period of music history ended around 1750. But already in the early 18th century a new simple style – the *style galant* – had grown up in France. This eventually undermined the more serious Baroque styles, and paved the way for the music of the Classical period. (*Galant* came from the Old French verb *galer* meaning 'to make merry'. The related German word *Galantieren* is sometimes used for the lighter, more 'modern' dances such as minuets and gavottes which come between the sarabande and gigue in a suite.)

With the *style galant* light tunefulness, delicate ornamentation, and regular phrasing (based on the dance) came to the fore. In fact, as Louis XIV's 72-year reign drew to a close, grandeur gave way to elegance and lightness in all the arts. The term 'rococo' is sometimes used, for example when referring to the paintings of Antoine Watteau (1684–1721), the designs of Nicolas Pineau (1684–1754) and the music of François Couperin. The term rococo probably combines the beginning of the French word *rocaille* ('shell': shell-like decorations were much loved in rococo architecture) and the ending of *barroco*.

The *style galant* spread to Germany, and eventually a more expressive form of it, known as the *empfindsamer Stil*, (German for 'sensitive, or sentimental style') was developed in the mid-18th century, notably by Bach's sons Wilhelm Friedemann (1710–1784) and Carl Philipp Emanuel.

Wilhelm Friedemann and Carl Philipp Emanuel Bach

The *style galant* and the *empfindsamer Stil* are sometimes referred to as pre-Classical styles because they preceded the Classical style that was seen to perfection in the work of Franz Joseph Haydn (1732–1809) and Wolfgang Amadeus Mozart (1756–1791).

The main Baroque instrumental genres (apart from suites of dances) survived into the Classical period. Instrumental music in fact became more dominant as, apart from opera, vocal music declined. Church music attracted less attention as religious certainties were challenged more and more, and the power and authority of the church began to weaken.

Many sonatas for solo keyboard were composed, increasingly for piano not harpsichord. Trio sonatas died out – string quartets (sonatas for two violins, viola and cello) were a kind of replacement. Concertos were almost all for solo instrument (usually piano or violin) plus orchestra. Symphonies, one of whose ancestors was the Italian overture (see end of Chapter 16), became the leading form of orchestral music.

The basso continuo system gradually wasted away, although a keyboard player still sometimes provided an improvised accompaniment, most vitally in *secco* recitative (as in Mozart's operas). Counterpoint did not vanish, but many lighter classical textures were basically 'melody-plus-bass', with the bass part little more than a simple harmonic support for a dominant melody line. (History sometimes repeats itself! Do you remember how at the start of the Baroque era counterpoint was very unpopular with some composers?) Harmonic rhythm accordingly tended to be slower and there was a growing emphasis on the two chords most vital in defining a key, I and V.

> Harmonic rhythm means the rate at which chords change. For example, where chords change rapidly, the harmonic rhythm is fast.

Periodic phrasing (where phrases are regular in length, in two-, four- and eight-bar units, and clearly balanced) became the basis of musical construction in place of the more continuous and irregular structure of much Baroque music. Binary form, as used for Baroque dances and some sonata movements, was extended into 'sonata form', the most important form of the Classical period and one which continued to have enormous influence in the 19th century and beyond. Fundamentally the same structure underlies a short Baroque minuet and the vast first movement from Symphony No. 3 in E♭ (the *Eroica*) by Ludwig van Beethoven (1770–1827).

Most important of all perhaps, the prolonging of a single affection throughout a movement was abandoned in favour of more rapid contrasts of mood and dynamic.

The 'Bach revival'

By the 1730s some people already considered the music of Bach to be hopelessly old-fashioned. Johann Adolph Scheibe (an important theorist and critic, and a minor composer, 1708–1776) criticised him for bewildering listeners with too much counterpoint, instead of writing more straightforward music in which it was clear which part carried the principal melody. Had Scheibe heard Bach's Air in D (FBC: 2)? There's no difficulty in hearing the melody of that piece – although Scheibe may have found it over-elaborate (judging from other comments he made about Bach's music).

Despite the misgivings of Scheibe and some others, Bach's music continued to be appreciated by small numbers of connoisseurs attracted by his outstanding contrapuntal skill.

In the early 19th century more and more people began to realise that Bach was not just a clever writer of counterpoint, but an outstanding composer in every respect. One major event was the performance in 1829 of the *St Matthew Passion* in Berlin, with the composer Felix Mendelssohn (1809–1847) conducting.

More and more of Bach's music was published (most of it had not appeared in print in his lifetime). The *Bach-Gesellschaft* (Bach Society) was founded in 1850, 100 years after the composer's death, in order to publish *all* his work (achieved in 1900).

The 'Bach revival' was important because, for the first time ever, the work of a neglected composer from the past was again heard widely. This kind of rediscovery was part of a new historical awareness which affected all the arts. Together, many similar but lesser musical rediscoveries opened up the vast array of musical styles (going back to the Renaissance and earlier) which people today take for granted. Take, for example, the early 20th-century rediscovery of the Elizabethan madrigal, something influential for many English composers, including Ralph Vaughan Williams (1872–1958) and Michael Tippett (1905–1998).

New music from old

The 'Bach revival' influenced composers as well as performers and listeners. For example, Robert Schumann (1810–1856) and Franz Liszt (1811–1886) both wrote organ works on the name of Bach, following Bach's own practice. Schumann's six fugues on B–A–C–H date from 1845, Liszt's Prelude and Fugue from between 1855 and 1870.

Old music had an even bigger influence on new in the 20th century, particularly from the 1920s to the early 1950s. The new music that resulted is often called 'Neoclassical' even when, as often happened, the old influences were Baroque and not Classical. ('Neoclassical' originally meant in a style based on the art or architecture of ancient Greece and Rome. Nowadays it can mean any revival of an earlier style in the arts. The prefix 'neo-' means 'in a new form', for any elements from previous styles normally exist alongside more up-to-date ones.)

Igor Stravinsky (1882–1971) was the leading Neoclassical composer. His ballet *Pulcinella* (1919–1920) was an orchestration and adaptation of little-known 18th-century Baroque music – for example, the Gavotte with two variations was based on a piece by Carlo Ignazio Monza (died 1739).

Birmingham Royal Ballet staging of Stravinsky's *Pulcinella*

But most Neoclassical works by Stravinsky were not modelled closely on specific pieces, and the influence of Baroque music is relatively slight. For example, the *Dumbarton Oaks* Concerto in E♭ for chamber orchestra (1937–1938) may remind you of a *Brandenburg* concerto from time to time – notice the continuous and energetic rhythms at the start and occasional melodic similarities – but the differences are far greater, not least in terms of harmony.

Some composers were greatly fascinated with Baroque forms. Dmitri Shostakovich (1906–1975) took Bach's *Das wohltemperierte Clavier* as the starting-point for his 24 Preludes and Fugues, Op 87 (1950–1951), as did Paul Hindemith (1895–1963) for *Ludus tonalis* (1942). Hindemith's title is Latin, meaning 'the tonal game' or 'the game of tonality'. His sub-title was 'studies in counterpoint, tonal organization and piano playing'.

Among the most original products of Neoclassicism were the nine *Bachianas brasileiras* (1930–1945) by the Brazilian composer Heitor Villa-Lobos (1887–1959). Many movements have both a Bach-style title and a Brazilian one: for instance *Bachianas* No 2 ends with 'Toccata: o trenzinho do Caipira' ('Toccata: the peasant's little train'). Here and elsewhere echoes of Bachian harmonic and contrapuntal idioms are fused with Brazilian rhythmic styles and timbres. Villa-Lobos conceived these works, often in suite form, as a homage to Bach, whom he regarded as of universal importance.

Baroque music has occasionally influenced writers of popular music (as we saw earlier with Pachelbel's Canon in D). A particularly fascinating case is Procul Harum's *A Whiter Shade of Pale* (1967) where some people hear echoes of Bach's Air in D, and of his 'Wachet auf' from Cantata No. 140. Jacques Loussier's trio has performed many jazz improvisations based on Bach's music (including the *Brandenburg* concertos). The

Swingle Singers, founded in the 1960s by Ward Swingle, have recorded a number of Bach's instrumental works using a kind of scat singing with nonsense syllables somewhat in the manner of Louis Armstrong.

For more examples of pop-classics correspondences, see http://www.allegro. philharmonic.me.uk/pach-can.htm.

The Swingle Singers in 2009

Performing Baroque music today

Most musicians would agree that performances by Loussier and the Swingle Singers are flights of fancy far from what Bach himself expected. But that agreement leaves open the question of quite what Bach and other Baroque composers *did* expect to hear. Believing that we owe it to them to play and sing their music as closely to what they intended as we can, some have become involved in period performances. These are performances that aim to recapture Baroque practice.

You may also meet the expressions 'historically-informed performance', or 'authentic performances', or just 'early music'.

The historically-minded performer must think about:

■ Original performing forces
■ Use of period instruments

- Performing technique
- Pitch and temperament
- Supplying features not in the score
- Interpreting what *is* in the score
- Writings on performance by Baroque musicians.

Let's consider each of the above headings in turn.

Original performing forces are the instruments and/or voices that Baroque composers would have expected to hear (where these differ from present-day resources), and the types and sizes of ensembles. For example, Bach played his French suites on harpsichord or clavichord, not piano, and Baroque choirs and orchestras were usually quite small.

Concerning use of period instruments – a closely related matter – performers need to consider if it is practical to play on instruments that have survived from Baroque times or (much more likely) on modern copies.

Performing technique concerns include, for example, the bowing of stringed instruments. In Baroque times Italian violinists often simply alternated upward and downward bow movements, even if an up-bow fell on a strong beat. French players, on the other hand, preferred downbows on strong beats, realising (as modern players do) that the strength of a down-bow helps emphasise the strength of a strong beat. Baroque string players probably employed vibrato sparingly, for instance to emphasise important long notes. Keyboard players often used the thumb and little finger less than we do, and sometimes crossed one finger over another.

Baroque pitch was not always the same as present-day pitch (see for example page 40, concerning the pitch at which Pachelbel's Gigue in D was probably originally played). Instruments weren't tuned to the modern standard of equal temperament in which all semitone intervals are equal and all keys sound in tune. Some Baroque tuning came close to equal temperament but the mean tone system, for example, was noticeably different: certain keys sounded excellent, but those with many sharps and flats were unusable. (See comments on pages 35 and 39 about temperament and tuning.)

Interpreting the score of a Baroque piece can be difficult because of the need to supply features not in the score: composers didn't give detailed performance directions or even sometimes all the necessary notes. Performers need to fill in the blanks, for example, by providing an accompaniment to fit given bass figuring, by adding ornamentation or by supplying phrasing and articulation, including legato and staccato.

Interpreting what *is* in the score means, for example, interpreting ornament signs and certain commonly used rhythmic patterns. Ornament signs were common in much keyboard music, especially in France (listen again to DMBE 2: 12, for example). Couperin and Bach produced instructions on how to interpret ornament signs, but these don't make everything completely clear.

Other contemporary writings on music theory and practice are not always straightforward and don't give clear-cut solutions to every performance issue. It is very clear, however, that the performance of dotted rhythms often differed from what we're used to in more recent music. For example the dotted rhythm ♩. ♪ was apparently often played as ♩ ♪ when it was heard against a group of three triplet quavers. (See how the rhythms have been aligned in the quotation from Bach's 'Jesu, joy' in Chapter 18.)

It works especially well in French music, when you play the rhythm ♪♩, to prolong the dotted note and shorten the following note, to produce what's known as overdotting or double-dotting.

In some French music a pair of quavers could be played unevenly (*notes inégales*, French for 'unequal notes', is the technical term) with the first note longer than the second. Depending on circumstances, you could play ♪♩ or ♩♪ or something in between, according to taste.

Some present-day musicians are less than enthusiastic about period performances, for example Pierre Boulez and Daniel Barenboim. They ask how important it is to our understanding and enjoyment to get heavily involved in trying to revive past performance traditions. In any case, you can't recreate fully the experience of a Baroque audience. To do this, you'd have to find a venue from the right period in the right country furnished according to Baroque taste, insist that everyone wore period dress, and so on. In the end it's largely a matter of common sense: not many of us have harpsichords, for example, so it's often more practical to listen to, or play, Bach's music on the piano.

> There is an important place too for *arrangements* of Baroque music for all kinds of instruments (including modern ones like the saxophone). Without them, many players would have a much thinner repertoire.

To sum up, we can't *fully* reproduce the sound of a performance from the Baroque period. But there is much to be said for using original and reproduction instruments, and researching how Baroque musicians played them, in order to try to come as close as possible to what Bach, Handel and their fellow composers themselves heard – it's like trying to eavesdrop on history.

To be able to offer convincing period performances, players and singers need accurate printed editions. These are made by referring where possible to the composers' own manuscripts and to early copies. Editions which keep as close to the composer's originals as modern notation allows (without lots of additional expression marks, for instance) are called *Urtext* editions (German for 'original text').

Period performance – some musicians

A pioneer of period performance was Arnold Dolmetsch (1858–1940), who built examples of instruments previously considered obsolete (notably viols, lutes, recorders and harpsichords). Wanda Landowska (1879–1959) was perhaps the first to play continuo accompaniments on the harpsichord, and her solo playing did much to persuade people that the instrument wasn't just an inferior ancestor of the piano.

The following are among the many important musicians in the period performance movement from the 1950s onwards:

- Nikolaus Harnoncourt (born 1929), conductor, cellist and viol player; founded the Concentus Musicus of Vienna in 1953, one of the first period instrument ensembles
- Gustav Leonhardt (born 1928), harpsichordist and conductor from the Netherlands
- Frans Brüggen (born 1934), conductor and recorder player from the Netherlands
- Christopher Hogwood (born 1941), English harpsichordist and conductor; founded the Academy of Ancient Music in 1973.

Nikolaus Harnoncourt

Gustav Leonhardt

Frans Brüggen

Christopher Hogwood

At times period performance styles have been controversial. Gustav Leonhardt once said that 'maybe [our style] is all wrong; I don't know, it could be' (see B. D. Sherman's *Inside Early Music: Conversations with Performers*, Oxford University Press, 1997). In the end, you must judge for yourself. If a performance makes the music come alive, and makes you want to hear more, it can't be dismissed.

Red Priest are one of the more controversial, yet popular, early music ensembles performing today

22. WHAT NEXT?

Even after 21 chapters, much remains unsaid. In this short book we've had to be selective: Baroque music extends over 150 years or more, and there's an enormous amount of it. Towards the end of this chapter we give you just a few hints of what we've had to miss out.

But first here are some ways (listening, playing, reading and so on) in which you can build on the knowledge you've acquired from Chapters 1–21.

Listen

Listen to BBC Radio 3 and/or Classic FM, both of which broadcast lots of Baroque music. *Radio Times* gives listings, or you can visit http://www.bbc.co.uk/radio3 or http://www.classicfm.com. You can hear some programmes via both websites as well.

Many CDs can be loaned from libraries, or bought from record shops or online. Naxos Music Library gives online access to over 10,000 Naxos CDs; the CDs themselves are very reasonably priced. A great deal of Baroque music is now available online, via YouTube, iTunes and Spotify.

Remember that you needn't always listen to an entire long work in one go. There are CDs with highlights from great works such as Handel's *Messiah* (Naxos CD 8.553258) and Bach's *St Matthew Passion* (Naxos CD 8.554169) for example. Nevertheless, when you're ready, you can't do better than listen to such works complete. Look out for live concerts including Baroque music too.

Perform

Much Baroque music is not difficult to perform. If you play or sing, ask an instrumental or singing teacher what solo pieces might suit you, or browse the shelves of a good library or music shop. For example, if you play the piano, consider the series *Baroque Keyboard Pieces* (ABRSM, 1991–1992). The four books, edited by Richard Jones, rise from 'easy' to 'moderately difficult'. Richard Jones has also edited *Baroque Flute Pieces* (five volumes, ABRSM, 1995–1996) and *Baroque Violin Pieces* (four volumes, ABRSM, 1998).

What music for larger forces you can take part in will depend to some extent on the choirs and orchestras in your area. But don't forget that it's sometimes possible to adapt or re-arrange the music for whatever players or singers are available. For example, Corelli's trio sonatas can sound reasonably good with flutes in place of violins and a piano playing the bass part and the accompaniment.

You can get inside the music in a unique way by composing in a Baroque style yourself. In some advanced music courses this means reconstructing pieces by Baroque composers, for example by completing the harmonisation of a chorale melody in the style of J. S. Bach. Bach himself taught his pupils to do this (the first stage was adding alto and tenor parts to given soprano and bass parts, then pupils were taught to write their own bass parts).

A similar task is completion of a two-part dance by (for example) Handel or Corelli or of a two-part invention by Bach by adding a top or bottom part to a given bottom or top part. There are chapters on chorale harmonisation and two-part writing in *A2 Music Harmony Workbook* (Rhinegold, 2008).

Use the internet

Much of the best material on the internet comes from colleges and universities, public organisations, and publishers of books and recordings. For other sites, and if ever in doubt, ask someone whose opinion you can trust. What's available on the internet may change from time to time. Here are just a few suggestions:

Go to http://www.lebrecht.co.uk, where you can find several pages of manuscript music in various composers' own hands. Below is an example.

Bach's manuscript copy of the chorale prelude 'Der Tag, der ist so freudenreich'

The score above uses two types of notation: ordinary staff notation (but without a separate stave for the pedals as is usual in present-day organ scores), and, squeezed in at the bottom, the closing bars are given in a form of tablature sometimes used by German organists in Baroque times.

At http://www.jsbach.net/images/manuscripts.html you can see more manuscript music in Bach's hand.

To follow this up, go to http://athome.harvard.edu/programs/wolff/ for a lecture for university students on the rediscovery of 'lost' manuscripts by Bach and others by Professor Christoph Wolff of Harvard University, USA.

Make internet searches for information about arts other than music (for example 'Baroque architecture'). The search may produce http://www.nga.gov/exhibitions/2000/Baroque/splash.htm, with 'The Triumph of the Baroque: architecture in Europe 1600–1750', based on an exhibition in 2000 at the National Gallery of Art. Try also the online *Artcyclopedia*.

Read

Remember the advice – 'listen, read, listen again (and then if necessary reread and re-listen)'.

To begin with, don't be too ambitious. Start, for instance, with the notes in a CD booklet. DMBE includes a booklet of over 130 pages on Baroque music, with notes on composers, suggestions for further listening, a glossary, and so on. Why not listen to the CDs and read the booklet in parallel?

Finally, here's a list of books (some of which cover much else besides Baroque music). Items at or near the top of the list are the more straightforward. When using books, be selective. Use indexes. *Build on* what you know or have heard of already.

- D. Bowman, *Rhinegold Dictionary of Music in Sound* (3 volumes, Rhinegold, 2002). Useful dictionary, 3 CDs and annotated music scores.
- *The Oxford Companion to Music*, ed. A. Latham (OUP, 2002).
- J. P. Burkholder, D. J. Grout and C. V. Palisca, *A History of Western Music*, 7th edition (Norton, 2005). New edition of a well-known book (same title) by D. J. Grout.
- *Norton Anthology of Western Music*, ed. J. P. Burkholder and C. V. Palisca, 5th edition, vol. 1 (New York: Norton, 2005), with 12-CD set: *Norton Recorded Anthology of Western Music*.
- C. V. Palisca, *Baroque Music* (3rd edition, Prentice-Hall, 1991). One of a series of very useful books on musical history periods by these publishers.
- *Companion to Baroque Music*, ed. J. A. Sadie (Macmillan, 1990). Biographical dictionary, with guide to national traditions. Foreword by Christopher Hogwood.
- J. W. Hill, *Baroque Music: Music in Western Europe, 1580–1750* (Norton, 2005) and *Anthology of Baroque Music* (Norton, 2005). Both useful at university level. There is also a web supplement http://www.wwnorton.com/college/music/hill with scores in PDF format.
- *The New Grove Dictionary of Music and Musicians* (Macmillan, 2nd edition, 2001). Articles on composers are often easier to read than those on genres – or the article on Baroque music itself. A particularly interesting section deals with Bach's methods of composition ('Bach, §III: (7) Johann Sebastian Bach, §21: Methods of composition'). The *New Grove* is available online: schools and college can subscribe to this.
- M. Bukofzer, *Music in the Baroque Era* (Dent, 1947). For a long time the classic book on Baroque music, but other books are now more up-to-date.

There's more...

In Chapters 1–21 we had to ignore some composers altogether. You can find out who a few were by looking at the track listings of WEM, DMBE and FBC. They include the Dutch composer Jan Pieterszoon Sweelinck (1562–1621). Known chiefly today for his keyboard music, he was a vital link between the English keyboard composers of the late Renaissance and the north-German tradition that reached its peak in J. S. Bach.

Composers not represented in our compilation CDs or in Chapters 1–20 include the Italian Girolamo Alessandro Frescobaldi (1583–1643) and his German pupil Johann Jacob Froberger (1616–1667). Frescobaldi, a keyboard virtuoso based largely in Rome, was the leading early Baroque composer of keyboard music. He was the first important composer to devote himself almost entirely to instrumental music – a sign of the gradual but accelerating shift from vocal music to instrumental music in the 17th and 18th centuries. Froberger likewise concentrated on keyboard music. He was an early pioneer of the suite (his Suite No. 2 already has the allemande–courante–sarabande–gigue format) and an important influence on later French and German keyboard writing.

We have had to be very selective in referring to specific pieces. One fascinating work that we cannot close without mentioning is Monteverdi's *Combattimento di Tancredi e Clorinda* ('The battle of Tancred and Clorinda') of 1624. The story is from a long poem about the late 11th-century First Crusade by Torquato Tasso (1544–1595), entitled *La Gerusalemme liberata* ('Jerusalem freed'), 1580. The tragic battle between two lovers is brought alive by one of the earliest uses ever of string tremolo and of pizzicato, vivid dynamics and many other descriptive touches. Monteverdi's *Combattimento* was included in his eighth book of madrigals (1638). Because it's long and unusually dramatic for a madrigal, modern writers have variously compared it to a secular cantata or oratorio, or an extended scene from an opera.

A modern staging of Monteverdi's *Combattimento di Tancredi e Clorinda*

It's not surprising that we don't always know how to classify Baroque works. Composers don't exactly make it easy for us: they aren't much concerned about labelling things uniformly. For them – as hopefully for us today – it's the *sound* of the music that really matters.

Epilogue

There is no time machine that will allow us to travel back in time to hear Bach play the organ or to have lessons in harmonising chorales from the master himself. We can't go back to the 1720s or 1730s to watch the first performances of Handel's operas (and see all the squabbling between soloists before they delighted their listeners). Nor can we catch the reactions of the first audiences to the 'modern' music of Monteverdi and Gabrieli. How new and shocking this must have seemed. Imagine the tut-tutting from elderly Italian churchmen and aristocrats: 'What on earth was wrong with Palestrina?'

What all of us *can* do is use to the full what we've got here and now – the hundreds of recordings and many scores will help us to gain a fuller understanding of this truly remarkable period of music history than we had 22 chapters ago.

GLOSSARY

This glossary is not comprehensive: it refers to terms as used in this book. A word in **bold** in a glossary entry refers you to an entry for another related word.

For fuller information about terms relating to tonality and harmony, see the AS Harmony Workbook and/or the A2 Harmony Workbook (Rhinegold, 2008). For fuller definitions of other terms and expressions, consult the Dictionary of Music in Sound by David Bowman (Rhinegold, 2002) and/or The New Grove (2001).

Accompaniment. In a **homophonic** texture, the parts that go with the main melodic part, providing the harmony and additional interest.

Adagio. (1) Tempo marking meaning 'slow' or sometimes just 'leisurely' or 'easy-going'. (2) A **movement** with Adagio as tempo marking.

Affection. An emotion or mood that lasts throughout a piece of music. Derived from German Affekt = 'emotion' or 'mood'.

Air. A song, or a piece with a songlike melody. In England and France, the word sometimes corresponded with the Italian word **aria**.

Allegro. (1) Tempo marking meaning 'quick' or sometimes just 'moderately quick' (the Italian word means 'cheerful'). (2) A movement with Allegro as tempo marking.

Allemande. A piece derived from a dance of German origin (usually in a suite the first or second movement). Generally moderate or reasonably slow, in $\frac{4}{4}$ time, with a short upbeat and plenty of gentle semiquaver movement.

Anthem. A type of piece, used in Church of England services, for choir (sometimes with soloists). Often accompanied by organ, occasionally by larger forces. Usually with English words (often from the Bible).

Antiphonal. Adjective describing music that uses **antiphony**.

Antiphony. Contrast between one group of performers and another.

Appoggiatura. A **dissonant** note sounding on the beat, usually for expressive effect, and resolving by step up or down to a consonant (harmony) note. An appoggiatura is not held over or repeated from the previous beat like a **suspension**, but approached from a different note, often by leap.

Aria. A song, usually from an opera, oratorio, Passion or cantata, for solo voice, plus accompaniment (which may be just for **continuo**). An aria often provides an opportunity for the singer to convey a particular **affection** at length. See also **Da capo aria**, **Recitative**.

Arioso. A section or piece that is part way between an **aria** and a **recitative** in manner of text-setting and level of musical interest.

Articulation. In music (as in speech) articulation aids clarity of delivery and coherence. Separating one note from the next by playing it **staccato** is a principal means of articulation in music. See also **Phrasing**.

Ballad opera. A play with English words (normally comic or farcical) that included short songs often based on traditional or popular tunes.

Ballet. A form of dance for the theatre without singing or speech but with scenery and costumes.

Basso continuo. *See* **Continuo**.

Binary form. A type of musical structure with two balancing sections, each usually repeated. The first generally ends in a key other than the **tonic**; the second ends in the tonic. Binary form was widely used in Baroque music, especially in dance movements.

Bourrée. A piece derived from a dance of French origin (when it appeared in a suite it usually came between the sarabande and gigue). Usually quick, and in ¢ or $\frac{2}{2}$ time with a crotchet upbeat.

Cadence. A pair of chords marking the end of a phrase. Cadences are of several types, of which perfect and imperfect are the most common. *See also* **Imperfect cadence, Perfect cadence, Phrygian cadence**.

Canon. A strict form of **imitation**, often lasting for an entire section or piece. The second voice or instrument to enter is an exact (or almost exact) copy of the first, although perhaps at a different pitch.

Cantata. Usually a work for voice(s) and instruments in several movements. A cantata is generally shorter than an oratorio, sometimes without chorus, and can be sacred or secular (non-church). In the early Baroque, 'cantata' (Italian for 'sung') was a rather vague term that could signify more or less any sung piece. *See also* **Oratorio**.

Canzona. A type of instrumental piece (mainly from the 16th and early 17th centuries) that is an important ancestor of the **sonata**.

Chamber. A room in a private house or palace, which could be small or large (as opposed to a *public* concert hall). *See also* **Da camera**.

Chorale. A type of German hymn sung in the Lutheran (Protestant) church from the time of the 16th-century Reformation. The word 'chorale' can refer to the melody only, or to the whole hymn.

Chorale prelude. *See* **Organ chorale**.

Chordal. *See* **Homophonic**.

Chorus. A movement for choir – usually with instrumental accompaniment. Can also mean a choir – the people who sing a chorus.

Chromatic. Generally, a chromatic note is outside the scale of the key or mode currently in use; for example, in G major C♯ and A♭ are chromatic. Movement in semitones is termed chromatic (e.g. the G–F♯–F–E♮–E♭–D of Purcell's 'When I am laid in earth'). An entire passage may be termed chromatic if it contains many chromatic notes.

Clavier. General term for keyboard instrument (without specifying harpsichord, clavichord, etc.).

Compound time. For example $\frac{6}{8}$ time, with the main beat subdivided into three equal parts. Opposite of simple time, where the beat has two equal parts (e.g. in $\frac{2}{4}$).

Glossary

Concertato style. Concertato style, used mainly in the first half of the 17th century, involved contrasts between different groups of performers, usually both vocal and instrumental. Basso **continuo** is always present. *See also* **Concerto**.

Concertino. The group of soloists in a Baroque **concerto grosso** – most commonly two violins and a cello (as in Corelli's Op. 6 concertos).

Concerto. From the late 17th century a concerto was usually a work for one or more solo instrumentalists plus other players with a secondary (i.e. often easier, less showy) role. A **concerto grosso** has three (very occasionally more) soloists, as opposed to a single soloist in a **solo concerto** or two soloists in a **double concerto**. An **orchestral concerto** has no clear distinction (or a less consistent one) between soloist(s) and others, although some sections may be more elaborate than others. (In the early Baroque 'concerto' meant a work in which voices and instruments, with more or less independent parts, collaborated, something fairly novel at the time.)

Concerto grosso. *See* **Concerto, Concertino, Ripieno**.

Continuo. Short for 'basso continuo' (Italian = 'continuous bass'). Refers to an instrumental bass line, most commonly for string(s) plus an improvised accompaniment on keyboard or lute that supplies full harmony that might otherwise be lacking.

Contrapuntal. Adjective to describe music that uses **counterpoint**.

Cori spezzati. Italian for 'separated choirs' (i.e. different groups of performers in different parts of a building), normally used in **antiphony**. *See also* **Coro**.

Cornett. A wind instrument made of wood with a cup mouthpiece. No connection with the modern brass cornet (single 't').

Coro. A group of performers, not necessarily singers, even though the Italian word 'coro' is from the same root as the English word 'choir'.

Counterpoint. (the adjective is **contrapuntal**). Counterpoint involves two or more melodic lines, usually rhythmically contrasted and each significant in itself, that are played or sung together (in contrast to **homophonic** writing).

Courante. A piece derived from a dance popular in the 17th century (usually in a suite the second or third movement). Quick or fairly quick, in $\frac{3}{4}$ or $\frac{3}{2}$ time. There is a distinction between a French type of courante and the lighter more dance-like Italian corrente.

Da camera. For the chamber. *See* **Chamber** and **Sonata**.

Da capo aria. An **aria** with a **ternary** structure. The music of the first section is repeated at the end of the second (often with the direction 'da capo', meaning '[repeat] from the beginning').

Da chiesa. For the church. *See* **Sonata**.

Diatonic. Opposite of **chromatic**. A diatonic note belongs to the scale of the key or mode currently in use (for example in G major the diatonic notes are G, A, B, C, D, E, F♯. In passages described as diatonic all or most notes are diatonic.

Diminished-7th chord. A **dissonant** four-note chord made up of superimposed minor 3rds, often used at moments of special intensity.

Dissonance. Any note that is not consonant (i.e. a major or minor 3rd or 6th, perfect 5th, unison or perfect octave above the lowest part). Some dissonances, particularly **suspensions** and **appoggiaturas**, add harmonic tension, and can represent sad or painful emotions; others, notably most passing notes (which just fill in gaps between neighbouring consonant notes) provide rhythmic and melodic decoration.

Dissonant. Adjective formed from the noun **dissonance**.

Double. Doubling occurs when two different instrumental and/or vocal parts share the same notes (either throughout a piece or section or more briefly).

Double concerto. *See* **Concerto**.

Double stopping. The playing of two notes simultaneously on adjacent strings of a string instrument. The term is sometimes used loosely to cover three- and four-note multiple stopping. *See* **Multiple stopping**.

Duet. An **aria** for two solo singers.

Dynamics. The 'louds and softs' in music, and the markings (such as f) used in some Baroque pieces to indicate them.

Edition. An edition sets out a piece in a manner convenient and clear for anyone who wants to perform or study it. Editions of Baroque music are necessary because some aspects of 17th- and early 18th-century notation are now unfamiliar, incomplete or unclear.

Ensemble. (1) A song for more than two soloists (especially in an opera). (2) A group of players and/or singers.

Episode. In a **rondeau** or in **ritornello form**, a section other than the refrain or ritornello section.

Fantasia. A term that implies an unusually great element of freedom, imagination and showiness (compare the related words 'fancy' and 'fantasy'). However it covers so wide a variety of pieces that no single definition fits all examples. Purcell's fantasias, which come at the end of a long English tradition of music for a group (or 'consort') of viols, have several short sections strongly contrasted in pace and texture. Bach sometimes paired a fantasia (instead of a prelude) with a fugue; although a fantasia may be more showy than a prelude there is no clear-cut difference.

Figured bass, Figures, Figuring. A figured bass is an instrumental bass part with 'figures' or 'figuring' (chiefly numerals and sharp, flat and natural signs) designed to show a continuo keyboard or lute player what type of chord to play. For example, 6 means 'play the **first inversion** of a **triad**', and ♯ means '**root position** triad with 3rd above bass sharpened'. A note without any figuring generally required a root position triad without accidental.

First inversion. When a chord has a note other than the root in the lowest part, it is an inversion. In a first inversion chord the 3rd of the chord is in the lowest part. For example, a chord of C major (C–E–G, with root C) is E–G–C in first inversion. A first inversion can also be termed a 6/3, because it has the intervals of a 6th and a 3rd above the lowest sounding note. *See also* **Root position**.

Glossary

Form. The overall structure of a movement. Types of form widely employed by Baroque composers include **binary form** and **ritornello form**.

French overture. *See* **Overture**.

Fugal. *See* **Fugue**.

Fugue. A type of piece in which a melody called the 'subject' is treated in **imitation** by all the parts (usually with short free passages for relief and contrast). The adjective is **fugal** (for instance, 'in fugal style' means 'in the style of a fugue').

Functional harmony. A type of harmony that has the function of defining a major or minor key, most of all through chords on the tonic and dominant (I and V), with special emphasis on **perfect cadences**.

Galliard. A dance movement, often in quick triple time, particularly popular in the 16th century. Often played after a **pavan**, a slower dance in duple or quadruple time. The pavan-galliard pairing was a forerunner of the Baroque **suite**.

Gavotte. A piece derived from a dance popular at the French court in the 17th century. In a suite it usually came between the Sarabande and Gigue. Generally of moderate speed, in ₵ time, often with a two-crotchet upbeat.

Genre. A type of musical work. Baroque genres include sonata, concerto and oratorio.

Gigue. A piece whose ancestor is the jig, a dance of British origin. In a suite it normally comes at the end. Quick and lively, and generally in $\frac{12}{8}$ or other compound time.

Ground bass. A melodic phrase used repeatedly in the bass over which the composer devises varied upper part(s). A ground bass is often heard at the same pitch throughout a piece, but it may be transposed.

Harmonisation. The provision of appropriate chords for a given melody.

Historia. In Protestant areas of Germany, a setting of a section of the Bible (especially one of the New Testament accounts of the sufferings and death of Jesus Christ). *See also* **Passion**.

Homophonic. Adjective to describe music that uses homophony (as opposed to **counterpoint**). One part has a melody while the others accompany, or all parts move together in **chordal** fashion (i.e. in the same or very similar rhythm).

Imitation. Where a melodic idea in one part is immediately repeated in another (exactly or inexactly), at the same or a different pitch, while the first part continues.

Imperfect cadence. An 'open-ended' or inconclusive **cadence** ending with the dominant chord (V). The preceding chord is usually I, II or IV. *See also* **Phrygian cadence**.

Improvise. To perform music that has not been notated in full or at all – in effect, to compose and perform simultaneously. Those who improvise often base their work on some existing musical material (e.g. when a keyboard continuo player plays from a **figured bass**).

Inventions. Two sets of 15 short **contrapuntal** pieces for keyboard by J.S. Bach. One set is in two-part counterpoint, the other in three.

Italian overture. *See* **Overture**.

Key. The type of **tonality** based on major and minor scales. A major key is based on a major scale, a minor key on a minor scale.

Largo. (1) Tempo marking meaning slow or slowish (the Italian word means 'broad'). (2) A movement with Largo as tempo marking.

Madrigal. Madrigals are normally secular (non-church) songs, often about love in a country setting. Most are for unaccompanied voices, but some from Monteverdi's time have basso continuo and perhaps other instruments.

Magnificat. Words of the Virgin Mary before the birth of Jesus (Luke, chapter 1) – widely used in church services. 'Magnificat' is the first word of the Latin version; the English version commonly begins 'My soul doth magnify the Lord'.

Mass. The Mass (with upper-case M) is the principal act of worship of the Roman Catholic church; it corresponds in some ways with communion or eucharistic services in other churches. A mass (often with lower-case m) is a musical setting of certain texts from the Mass (generally including 'Kyrie eleison' and 'Gloria in excelsis').

Melisma. A group of notes on a single syllable, often for expressive purposes or **word-painting**.

Melismatic. Adjective from noun **melisma**.

Minuet. A piece derived from a dance of French origin (in a suite it usually came between the sarabande and gigue). In $\frac{3}{4}$ time, and generally graceful and not very fast. A minuet was normally played through twice, before and after a 'trio' (another minuet in all but name).

Modes. Scales from which major and minor scales evolved. Ancestors of the major scale (with a major 3rd above the first note of the mode) are the Ionian, Lydian and Mixolydian modes. These employ all the white notes within one octave on a keyboard, starting respectively on C, F and G. Ancestors of the minor scale (with a minor 3rdabove the first note) are the Dorian, Phrygian and Aeolian modes. These employ all the white notes within one octave, starting on D, E and A.

Modulation. The process of changing key, or simply a change of key.

Monody. A term used nowadays to describe music for single voice plus continuo of the novel text-dominated type devised in Italy c.1600. An early 17th-century term was *stile rappresentativo*, meaning representational or dramatic style.

Motet. A type of church music for choir (or solo voice), sometimes accompanied by organ, sometimes by larger forces. A motet usually has Latin words, often from the Bible, and is associated (chiefly but not only) with Roman Catholic worship.

Motif. A short but distinctive musical idea that is developed in various ways to create a longer passage of music.

Movement. A movement is a piece within a piece. Unlike a section, it is usually complete in itself, and can be played on its own.

Multiple stopping. The term covers 'triple stopping' (the simultaneous playing of three notes on adjacent strings of a string instrument) and 'quadruple stopping' (playing of four notes as near to simultaneously as possible on all four strings). *See* **Double stopping**.

Glossary

Obbligato. In an **aria**, an obligatory (that is, essential) solo instrument in addition to the vocal part and continuo. It has an independent melodic part that features in the opening **ritornello** and afterwards is only slightly less important melodically than the solo part itself. (Italian: 'necessary', 'obligatory'.)

Opera. A large-scale dramatic work for singers and instrumentalists. In most cases the whole text is sung, so that an opera is very different from a play with incidental music. *See also* **Ballad opera**, **Semi-opera**.

Oratorio. A work with religious words for singers and instrumentalists, in various movements. Often on a very large scale. *See also* **Cantata**, **Passion**.

Orchestral concerto. *See* **Concerto**.

Organ chorale. An organ piece based on a **chorale** melody. Also often known as a **chorale prelude** (although that term is sometimes limited to shorter settings intended to introduce a chorale which the congregation then sang).

Ornamentation. Addition of melodic decoration, often through the use of conventional ornaments such as trills and mordents.

Overture. An instrumental piece, usually in two or more sections of contrasting tempi, played before an opera or extended choral work. The opening of a **French overture** is slow, the opening of an **Italian overture** is quick. Overtures were sometimes composed and performed independently of larger vocal works.

Partita. Most commonly, an alternative name for a **suite**.

Passion. A musical setting of the story of the sufferings and death on the cross of Jesus Christ as told in one of the gospel accounts in the Bible. An oratorio Passion includes some non-Biblical words as well. A Passion oratorio tells the Passion story in verse.

Pavan. *See* **Galliard**.

Perfect cadence. A **cadence** ending with the tonic chord (I), preceded by the dominant (V) or dominant seventh (V^7) – the principal resource for establishing a key, and appropriate where some degree of finality is required.

Phrase. A number of notes that form a semi-independent part of a longer musical structure (compare, in speech or writing, a phrase within a sentence). Phrases are often between two and four bars long.

Phrasing. How the composer (or performer) divides a passage or section of music into **phrases**.

Phrygian cadence. A type of **imperfect cadence**, in which the dominant chord (V) is preceded by the first inversion of the subdominant (IVb). It is used chiefly in minor keys.

Pizzicato. Plucking, instead of bowing, string(s) on a violin, viola, cello or double bass.

Plainsong. Also known as plainchant. A type of music widely used in the Roman Catholic church from the earliest times. It is monophonic (i.e. with a single unharmonised melody), and has limited rhythmic variety.

Prelude. The first of a pair of substantial instrumental movements in the same key (e.g. 'prelude and fugue'), or sometimes the first movement in a sonata or suite. Although the parent Latin term 'praeludium' originally implied something brief and introductory, most Baroque 'preludes' are much more than this. *See also* **Organ chorale.**

Range (as in 'soprano range'). The interval between the lowest note and the highest in an instrumental or vocal part. For example, a soprano part which works between middle C and the G just above the treble stave has a range of an octave and a 5th.

Recitative. A piece for solo voice in an opera, cantata or oratorio in which clear projection of words is the main concern. In many recitatives the music is functional rather than of great interest in itself, with the accompaniment often just for **continuo.** A recitative often precedes an **aria.**

Register. A distinct part of the **range** of an instrument or voice (for example, the high clarino register of a trumpet).

Relative major. The major key with the same key signature as a specific minor key elsewhere in the piece. If a piece begins in D minor, for example, the relative major is F major: both keys have a signature of one flat.

Relative minor. Opposite of **relative major.** The relative minor of F major is D minor, for example.

Ripieno. Players other than soloist(s) and continuo in a Baroque concerto. (Italian for 'filling up' or 'completion'. It doesn't imply large numbers – there might be only one player to a part.)

Ritornello. (1) The opening section in **ritornello form,** and other sections that repeat some or all of the same material (perhaps in a different key). (2) An instrumental passage within a vocal item. (Italian for 'a little return' – i.e. a refrain.)

Ritornello form. A type of musical structure similar to **rondeau** but more sophisticated, because the opening ritornello section (which corresponds to the refrain in a rondeau) can appear in key(s) other than the tonic, and may be shortened or varied.

Rondeau. A type of piece of French origin in which an opening section in the tonic key alternates with other music. This opening section and its repeats can be called 'refrain' or 'rondeau' – or just A. The other sections are **episodes** or 'couplets'. The most common pattern is ABACA (or, with repeats, AABACAA).

Root position. A chord which has the root in the lowest sounding part. **Triads** in root position are sometimes termed 5/3s.

Sarabande. A piece derived from a dance of Spanish origin (in a suite usually the third or fourth movement). Generally slow and in triple time (notably $\frac{3}{4}$), often with the second beat of the bar emphasised.

Semi-opera. An English genre known today chiefly from the work of Henry Purcell (1659–1695). A kind of half-way house between play and opera: the principal characters have spoken parts; the others have parts with singing and dancing.

Sinfonia. An Italian word, literally meaning (like the related English word 'symphony') 'sounding together'. There are several distinct meanings: (1) an instrumental section or interlude in a work for voices and instruments; (2) an **overture** in an Italian opera (one of the ancestors of the Classical orchestral symphony); (3) 'concerto-sinfonia' is another name for an orchestral **concerto**; (4) Bach referred to his three-part **inventions** as 'sinfonias'.

Solo concerto. *See* **Concerto**.

Sonata. An instrumental piece, usually for one or a few players, and usually in three or four movements. Many Baroque sonatas are for single melody instrument and continuo. **Trio sonatas** are normally for two violins and continuo. A sonata **da chiesa** was for use in church and avoided movements with dance titles. A sonata **da camera** was for the **chamber**; it contained movements with dance titles, and had much in common with a **suite**. (In the early Baroque, 'sonata' meant little more than a piece that was played (literally 'sounded') not sung.)

Sonata form. A form developed in the Classical period from binary form. Much used for the first movements of symphonies and sonatas in particular.

Stile antico. Term of early 17th-century origin for church music that is still basically in the old-fashioned Renaissance style, with unaccompanied voices. (Italian: 'antique (or ancient) style'.)

Stile moderno. Term of early 17th-century origin for music which is not **antico**, but more up-to-date, for voices and basso continuo (with or without other instruments). (Italian: 'modern style'.)

Stile rappresentativo. *See* **Monody**.

String quartet. A chamber work from the Classical period or later. In effect a sonata for two violins, viola and cello, and usually in four movements.

Suite. A collection of pieces, mostly or entirely dances, usually all in the same key. (French: a 'succession' or 'series'.)

Suspension. A **dissonance** occurring at a change of chord. One part hangs on to (or repeats) a note from the old chord, thus creating the dissonance, after which the delayed part resolves by step (usually down) to a note of the new chord.

Symphony. The common meaning (from the second quarter of the 18th century onwards) is a work for orchestra with several movements, usually three or four in different tempi – in effect a sonata for orchestra. In English Baroque music it was sometimes similar in meaning to **ritornello** (2). Handel called the overture to *Messiah* 'Sinfony'. *See also* **Sinfonia**.

Te Deum. A Christian hymn in Latin prose dating from the 4th century. The opening words 'Te Deum laudamus' are often translated as 'We praise you, God'.

Tempo. The speed of a piece or passage of music. In a Baroque piece tempo is often obvious from the character or title, but it is sometimes indicated by a word such as **Allegro** or **Adagio**.

Ternary form. A type of musical structure with three sections, the first and last of which are the same or similar, the second providing contrast. A type of ternary form was widely used for **arias** in the Baroque period (*see* **Da capo aria**).

Texture. The relationship between the various simultaneous lines in a passage of music, dependent on such features as the number and function of the parts and the spacing between them.

Timbre. The characteristic sound quality of a voice or instrument – the timbre of a violin is different, for example, from the timbre of a trombone, even when they sound the same pitch.

Toccata. Most early Baroque toccatas are keyboard pieces, the Italian word 'toccata' meaning 'touched'. (The instrumental opening of Monteverdi's opera *Orfeo* is one of a number of exceptions.) In northern Europe in the late 17th-century an organ toccata had both showy passages that sound almost improvised and also fugal sections.

Tonality. Most often used for the system of keys based on major and minor scales that had evolved by about 1670 and was governed by **functional harmony**.

Tonic. (1) The main key of a piece or movement. (2) The note after which a key is named, and the first (and most important) of its scale (e.g. A is the tonic note of the key of A major). (3) The **triad** built on the tonic note – often referred to as chord I.

Triad. A type of three-note chord ('tri-' = 'three'). In its basic form (or in close **root position**) the top note is a 3rd above the middle note, which is a 3rd above the lowest note. *See also* **Inversion**.

Trio sonata. *See* **Sonata**.

Triplet. A group of three equal notes played in the time normally taken by two notes of the same type. For example, a triplet of quavers is played in the time of two ordinary quavers.

Versicle and response. In a church service, a versicle is a short sentence from the Bible which is sung by one unaccompanied voice. The following response has a related answering set of words sung by the choir (and/or congregation).

Vespers. (1) An afternoon or evening service of the Roman Catholic or Lutheran church ('Vespers' comes from the Latin for 'evening'). Corresponds in some respects to the Church of England service of Evening Prayer or Evensong. (2) Name of a musical setting of texts for such a service (notably Monteverdi's *Vespers*).

Vibrato. Where a singer or player repeatedly and deliberately changes the pitch or intensity of a note very slightly for expressive effect.

Vivace. (1) Tempo marking meaning 'lively'. (2) A movement with Vivace as tempo marking.

Voluntary. Most commonly a piece for organ played before or after a church service.

Word-painting. Where a composer makes the music illustrate a detail in the text, as when a descending interval or melody is used to represent the word 'fall'.

INDEX

*Principal entries for each heading are shown in **bold**.*

Index

PICTURE CREDITS

Cover image: The Royal Collection © 2010, Her Majesty Queen Elizabeth II

page 8: University of Texas Libraries
page 11: Lebrecht Authors
page 12: Private collection, London
page 13: Lebrecht Music & Arts
page 17: Superstock/Getty Images
page 19: Laurie Lewis/Lebrecht Music & Arts
page 21: Damil Kalogjera
page 29: Graham Salter/Lebrecht Music & Arts
page 32: Shestakoff/Shutterstock
page 34: Lebrecht Music & Arts
page 39: Edinburgh University Collection of Historic Musical Instruments
page 44: Lebrecht Music & Arts
page 45: Adrian Horsewood
page 46: Richard Haughton
page 54: Lebrecht Music & Arts
page 60: Lebrecht Music & Arts
page 64: Lebrecht Music & Arts
page 68: Lebrecht Music & Arts
page 73: Chris Christodolou/Lebrecht Music & Arts
page 80: VVO/Shutterstock
page 85: Lebrecht Music & Arts
page 86: Biblioteca del Conservatorio di Musica "G. B. Martini", Bologna
page 90: Joanne Harris/Lebrecht Music & Arts
page 97: Lebrecht Music & Arts
page 98: Lebrecht Music & Arts (Wilhelm Friedemann Bach, Carl Philipp Emanuel Bach)
page 101: Dee Conway/Lebrecht Music & Arts
page 102: Shutterstock
page 105: G. Anderhub/Lebrecht Music & Arts (Nikolaus Harnoncourt)
page 105: T. Martinot/Lebrecht Music & Arts (Gustav Leonhardt)
page 106: T. Martinot/Lebrecht Music & Arts (Frans Brüggen, Christopher Hogwood)
page 106: Martin Riedl (Red Priest)
page 108: Lebrecht Music & Arts
page 110: Patrick Riviere/Getty Images